Become Enlightened

The Meaning of Life

David William

ISBN 978-0-473-66699-6

This book is dedicated to my Angel, Karyn Wheeler

Table of Contents

Introduction

You at this very moment are playing a game. The most astonishing and extraordinary game that could ever be imagined. A game for the ages. A game to take your breath away. When I say "game" I am not using a metaphor. I mean that this life is literally a game designed by a higher power and you have been playing it your entire life.

On a personal or micro level, this is a game of twists and turns, of beautiful peaks and devastating lows. On the macro level everything is flawlessly calibrated and utterly perfect.

Nothing happens that is not meant to be. Every flap of a butterfly's wing is timed to perfection and is a precise component of the overall system.

This book is a handbook for the extraordinary game of life. It explains and describes the big picture. It describes the overarching themes and spiritual laws that govern this game of life. It gives you answers to the big questions. Real answers, not just whimsical words describing nothing. Find out……

Why is there something & not nothing?
Who am I & why am I alive?
Why are we playing this game?
What are the rules and the nature of the game?
What is my life purpose?
How do I stop the pain & emotional suffering I feel in my life?
What is spiritual enlightenment & how can I achieve it in clear steps?
How do I achieve perfect & long-lasting inner peace and happiness?
How does this universe actually operate at the galactic level?

(Note: In this book I use the words universe, multiverse and game interchangeably).

You will be astonished at how perfectly designed this game is. Your eyes will be opened and your mind awakened. Everything in the multiverse and beyond is working in harmony and you are a piece of it. You will discover how you fit in to the game of life. What your role as a player consists of, where you are now and where you could go. This book will give you the information you need to thrive and to flourish playing this game.

Chapter 1: The Big Picture is an introduction into the basics of spirituality. We will look at the spiritual laws of the game and how these laws affect you. You will see how spirituality and quantum physics come together to create this game we are all playing.

Chapter 2: The Egoic Self explains that you are not who you think you are. You have been deceived by your ego. It explains how you can begin to wake up and realise your divine nature, breaking free from the ego's control and the emotional pain and suffering which comes from it.

Chapter 3: We Are Living in a Computer Simulation explains and provides evidence that this life we experience is actually holographic and part of a very powerful computer simulation.

Chapter 4: Become Spiritually Enlightened will explain how you can realise the truth of being spiritually enlightened. It will outline real steps in plain English, not religious babble, that will lead you towards the ultimate achievement in life. Once achieved everything changes. You will experience bliss, peace and happiness.

Chapter 5: The Meaning of Life explains exactly why you are playing this game and what you are here to do. I will literally explain in detail the true meaning of life. This chapter also explains how the universe is ordered at the galactic level and where we fit in. Find out how highly evolved beings live in other parts of the universe, the powers they have and how much more evolved they are compared to us.

Chapter 1
The Big Picture

The first of the big questions

I would like to start this book by posing a question to you.

What is your essence?

Take a minute to ponder this before reading on.

People generally have no idea how to even begin to answer this question. The usual response is a scratch of the head and a vacant stare before coming up completely blank. Some people will throw up their name, their sex or even their nationality in a hopeful attempt to put their finger on it. But does this come close to answering the question of who and what they really are?

It's a fact that most people live their entire life (play the entire game) without even thinking about this question. The fact that you have chosen this book means you are not like most people. If you are reading this book, it means you are ready. You are ready to finally know the truth.

This is a big question. It is a question of identity at the most fundamental and basic level.

To answer this question, we must look within. Once again this is something that a lot of people just don't want to do. People often see themselves rather superficially. They care more for entertainment or how many likes or loves they have garnered from social media.

It's often only when the game gets really hard that people do suddenly look within and try to find some meaning. But why wait for an existential crisis to happen before you answer this question? Let's do it now and hopefully we won't need our world to fall apart before we find meaning.

Where almost everyone on the planet goes wrong, is that they believe they are a separate human being with their own separate body and their own separate mind. It sounds obviously true doesn't it? But it's not. It is completely wrong. This is the great illusion. The wool has been pulled over our eyes. Very simply you are not at all what you think you are. The illusion of you being a separate human being is necessary for you to be able to play this extraordinary game we call life. It may be necessary, but it is still a total illusion.

So, who are you if you are not a human being? The correct answer is that your essence is God. Not metaphorically, but literally. You are literally God. Not just part God either. You are the big guy in the sky himself. Or if you prefer the big woman herself. It doesn't matter as God is equally feminine and masculine.

I'm not saying you are a human being with a soul either, because that would mean your essence is human. This is what a lot of religious people think. They think they are a human being who will have a spiritual experience when they die. In truth the reverse is true. You are a spiritual being (God) having a temporary human experience. The human part of you is very much temporary. Most people are lucky if they live past 90. While on the other hand your spiritual life lasts forever. You are immortal.

Being God

Some people may find this proposition that they are God as being very unlikely. They, in most probability certainly don't feel like God. They don't seem to have any special powers for one thing. How many people in the world can conjure up a simple miracle like turning water into wine for example? Or how about parting the ocean when you go swimming? Most human beings don't back themselves to pull off such a miracle.

They very much feel and experience that which is called the human condition. They have limitations. They have character faults. Most people have a number of problems or issues in playing this game. It could be serious illness. It could be addictions. It could be lack of money or an unfulfilling career. It could be anything. But despite all these problems and despite the human condition, everyone is God.

Many people, especially religious folk, might say claiming to be God is blasphemy. Christians are taught that Jesus is God incarnate and that we are not. So, let's look closer at this. Christians believe that Jesus was the son of God. The term "son" when translated properly does not mean he was literally God's son, as in offspring. It means Jesus was godlike. It means Jesus' essence was the same as God. We have already established that our essence is God. So, by this reasoning we are all like Jesus.

The big difference was Jesus knew he was God and had fully realised this fact. We just need to fully realise this truth and step into our divinity. Can we perform miracles like Jesus did? No, we can't, not yet. Jesus was far more highly evolved than we are. We are not at his level yet. But at some point, we will be at his level. It will take a number of lifetimes for this to happen. Yes, reincarnation is real, and it is a truth of the universe. I will explain more about reincarnation later in this book. But it's enough to know at this stage that we all evolve higher and higher with each incarnation.

Jesus could have incarnated in a place and time far more evolved than first century Earth, but he chose to lower his vibration and come here on a mission. A mission to, by way of example, show us the truth. To model for us what is possible when you know you are God at your essence. He did a remarkable job at this. Anytime a whole civilisation rewrites the record of time based on your life (BC & AD), you know you have had a pretty big impact!

It is my personal belief that all of us, just like Jesus, are divine beings. We have massive untapped potential. We could perform miracles ourselves if we just believed enough and didn't doubt how powerful we really are. This is what awaits us in future incarnations. We will be able to perform miracles and given time, we too, will be just as loving and just as powerful as the great spiritual master Jesus.

Religion has lied to you

So why were we not taught this at school? Why do so few people know who they really are? These are good questions. The answers are complicated and multifaceted but there is one main reason. That reason is religion.

Religion, especially the western religions did not want you to know you are God.

Take the Christian religions. If this knowledge that we are all divine was commonplace, do you think so many people would be practicing Christians and attend church regularly? Not likely and here is why. Right now, Christians are told that they are sinners. They are so frightened that they might go to hell when they die that they attend church on Sundays so that they can ward off this awful possible post life experience. The leaders of the Christian faiths from the past set it up just like this to keep their religions going. To get the number of people attending church as high as possible.

Over the centuries past, churchmen have edited religious books like the Bible so that most references to our divinity have been scrubbed out. Yes, I will say it again. The Bible has been heavily edited. Whole passages have been removed and new one's inserted. The reason they did this is because they wanted to recruit followers to their religion. To recruit followers, they wanted to paint us as human beings who are sinners. Then the rhetoric is that us sinners will go to everlasting hell when we die unless we have joined the ranks of the said religion.

They have set the whole situation up to be absolutely dreadful (everlasting hell) and the only way out is to join the team. If people knew the truth that they are God and that there is no such place as hell after we die the whole system would fall over. This is why it is so important to realise there is no place called hell in the afterlife. I repeat this a number of times in this book because it is this false and fictional place that religion talks about that causes emotional suffering to believers of these religions. The whole set up of many Christian religions revolves around sin and hell. They go hand and hand. This hurts people and it makes them afraid when they needn't be.

The Catholic religion has even gone as far as to state that every newborn baby is a sinner. Even a baby less than a day old is said to be a sinner. They call this original sin. This sin harks back to the creation story where Adam and Eve disobeyed God and ate an apple from the tree of knowledge of good and evil. The result of this was that original innocence was lost and all subsequent human beings are born into a state of sinfulness. The eating of the apple is the original sin and every baby born carries this sin. In these Christian faiths, the only way to have this sin lifted from your soul is of course to be baptised into that faith.

A baby one day old, has done nothing wrong. They are perfect in every way. They have not been conditioned by their family and by society, so they love themselves completely. There is no reason to be absolved of any sin. Yet that is what some of these Christian faiths teach.

Why would a loving God have the need to punish people by sending them to hell for an eternity? Is God that thin skinned and insecure? Only a narcissistic psychopath would be that cruel. If a person alive today used this form of torment and punishment to people under his control, he would be sent to prison. Yet so many people think it's reasonable for a soul to suffer for an eternity because they made some mistakes during their short life. God is obviously as highly evolved as you can get. Would this supreme being really have a need to inflict pain and suffering on one of his children? Not just for a short time but for ever? This is not the God that I believe in. However, this is the God that some Christian religions worship.

Hell does exist in a way, but it's not like many Christians believe. There is no place called hell, but hell exists as a state of mind when we are well and truly alive on this planet. We all have experienced "going through hell" from time to time. When we believe we are an individual separate from God and life gets really hard, that's when we are in hell. It is not so much what happens to us in life, its more how we react emotionally. We resist what happens and we get angry or become distraught. This is emotional suffering, and it is commonplace. We create this for ourselves because we resist life. We do not accept life and surrender to life. It's our negative feelings and negative emotions which lead us into hell on Earth. Conversely heaven can also be a state of mind. We all have beautiful, blissful moments at times too. People often go back and forwards from heaven to hell as they go through the game. More often than not, more time is spent in living hell than in heaven. There is a great quote from Winston Churchill; "If you feel like you are in hell, keep going."

I am not saying that all religions are bad. Not at all. There are many good things in all religions. I do personally believe however that the Eastern religions are more useful than the Western religions, but I don't really support the idea of joining a team when it comes to spirituality at all.

Spirituality is a deeply personal business. The idea of a huge group of people all believing the same thing and adhering to the same dogma just doesn't make sense to me. Just because you are born into a family who follow a certain religion, is that a good reason to commit yourself by default to that one religion for the rest of your life? It's like being born in a particular town or city. It's a big world out there. You don't need to live in the same town your whole life just because you were born there.

I do believe that much of the dogma in Christianity is restrictive. The treatment of women and people who are not heterosexual is poor. Christian religion has a lot of rules that members are expected to follow. No sex before marriage, no gay sex, no contraception (in some Christian religions).

The God I believe in does not have rules and allows us to be free to live any way we want especially if this makes us happy.

It is my belief that the Bible has been edited and a lot has been left out. Despite this there are still a few passages in the Bible that have survived the editing of these churchmen over the centuries and hint at the truth. One such passage is John 10:34 where Jesus quotes from Psalm 82:6 and says very simply "Ye are Gods." Another passage; John 10:34-35 "Is it not written in your law, I said, you are Gods?"

Another profound and beautiful passage from the Bible that was not left on the cutting room floor is known as the golden rule and it was proclaimed by Jesus during his sermon on the mount. It does not hint at our divinity, but it is very powerful. The English translation is "Do unto others as you would have done onto you." This golden rule has the power to change the world completely if it was taken up by most of the world's population. This is an example of the good that exists in religion.

So, the Bible still has some beautiful and powerful messages, but much has been lost. We may never know how much has been removed and how many passages have been altered. There are already several different versions of the Bible in print with different passages and different words. This very fact confirms that editing has taken place, so it is more a question of how much of it has taken place, rather than has it happened at all.

The Bible is actually a collection of writings or books as it is today. Often, we hear religious teachers quoting the more pleasant or enlightening quotes from it but they are cherry picking the Bible to find the best or more acceptable quotes. Some of the passages in it are straight out misogynistic/homophobic or they are extreme in terms of spelling out what is right or wrong and the punishment should you do such a wrong. It is black and white in terms of the way it dictates how one should live. Here is an example of such a passage from Luke 16:18 "Everyone who divorces his wife and marries another commits adultery, and he who marries a woman divorced from her husband commits adultery." Does the most evolved and loving being in creation (God) really feel so uptight about divorce? Does God really require couples to stay together their whole lives even if they are deeply unhappy? Another passage; Leviticus 20-13 "If a man also lie with mankind, as he lieth with a woman, both of them have committed an abomination: they shall surely be put to death." What kind of evolved God would say this? God requires a killing to take place just because two consenting men have sex? Is this not a stark contradiction to the well-known passage from Matthew 7:1 "Judge not, that ye be not judged." These two passages are completely contradictory.

Many people read the Bible and believe every word and it is a shame because not only does it make people very unhappy it can be the cause of actual wars between communities and even countries.

.

Advaita Vedanta

I have focused here on Christianity but there are some religions that teach the truth that we are all God. One of these is a philosophy that comes from the Hindu religion called Advaita Vedanta. In this Hindu philosophy the underlying fundamental reality of everything in existence is said to be God (Brahman). The term Advaita refers to the idea that Brahman (God) alone is real while the transient phenomenal world is an illusionary appearance of Brahman.

Of all the religions it is this form of Hinduism (Advaita Vedanta) that is most congruent with the teachings in this book. Buddhism teaches that there is no God. On the other hand, Advaita Vedanta teaches that everything we see in our world is God at its essence. That is the main difference between the two religions. However, both religions do agree that all the form we see all around us is actually an illusion. They also agree that it is the nature of life for human beings to suffer emotionally until they find liberation from suffering by achieving the state of enlightenment.

Before the game was created there was only God

You may be wondering, if I am really God what am I doing here in this body? This is a good question.

To answer this question, we must look at the very big picture. We must go all the way back in time to before the game even existed or before the game was created. Before the big bang itself. That is over 13.7 billion years ago. This is before the existence of all the things we have become used to. There were no galaxies, no stars, no planets, no people, no animals, nothing that is familiar to us.

At this time before the game even existed there was only one entity. That entity was God. Just God and nothing else. God in this expression was all powerful and all loving and she was ubiquitous. She was absolutely everywhere. We are not sure what form God took but most people visualise God existing as pure energy or pure consciousness. This pure energy or pure consciousness has some attributes which are inherent in it. For example, many people describe God as being pure love or pure light.

God created an extraordinary game

God in this expression had a problem though. The problem was that she was only experiencing pure love, pure joy, pure happiness, and the full gamut of other positive emotions. She wanted to experience more than this. She didn't know sadness for example. She knew happiness very well but how could she truly appreciate happiness if she didn't know its opposite. It was the same with Joy. She experienced utter Joy but she wanted to know misery so she could truly appreciate Joy. Also, her experience of life in this expression was very limited. There was only her and nothing else to interact with. She wanted to be able to experience life in a more complex and social way.

God got to realise that there were many possible experiences she was missing out on. She wanted to experience every possible thing she could regardless of whether it might be considered a positive or negative experience. So, to do this, God hatched a plan. Her plan was to create a game. An extraordinary game that would allow God to experience every single possible experience, emotion and feeling that could possibly exist. You guessed it. You are God playing that game right now!

The first thing God did was to divide herself up into many smaller pieces. For simplicity and consistency throughout this book let's call these smaller pieces of God "souls" and let's call God in her full expression "source." The word source is often used in spirituality because very simply God in her full expression is the source of everything in the game. We don't know how many souls were created but it could be a vast number perhaps even an infinite number of souls. Each soul is not as powerful as source but is nevertheless 100% divine and contains the same characteristics as source including creative power.

Source needed to have somewhere to send each soul, so she designed a game. She designed this extraordinary game that we call life. She literally created the big bang that started our own universe/game. She created big bangs for other universes as well. Possibly an infinite number of parallel universes/games. This act of creation is so incredible and so amazing that our brains cannot comprehend just how truly awe inspiring it was.

She made the game out of herself. You could say that everything in the game is made out of God stuff. Scientists tell us that at the big bang all the matter in the game was compacted into a very small space. In fact, the universe was once a singularity very dense and very tiny. This tiny but very dense matter is the God stuff everything is made out of. This God stuff exploded outwards from the big bang and later over time formed galaxies, stars, planets, oceans, mountains, people, animals, marine life, minerals, vegetation, everything in existence.

The game is full of life

It took time for matter to coalesce and to form what we see now.

We believe there could be as many as two trillion galaxies in our universe. In our galaxy the Milky Way alone, there is thought to be four hundred billion stars and at least one hundred billion planets. We think there could be as many as ten septillion planets in the observable universe. That written out in numbers is 10,000,000,000,000,000,000,000,000 planets. That is obviously an absolutely incredible number of planets. Even if only a small percentage of these planets are Earth like, it still means the game is likely teaming with life and again this is only the observable universe which could be just a tiny fraction of the entire universe. The entire universe could well be infinite in size.

So over time natural selection and evolution took place on Earth until our planet was as we see it now. Those souls that source created were sent out and embedded in the form we see around us. There are 8 billion human beings on the planet. Each of these people have a soul. Actually, it is more correct to say each person is a soul. Every creature on the planet from the smallest insect to a lion are all souls too. Even minerals in the Earth and vegetation on the Earth like trees and flowers are souls. Everything we see around us comes from that God stuff which exploded out from the big bang. Everything is divine. Everything is God.

The game is made out of pure consciousness

It goes further than that though. Every form has a divine spark of consciousness or awareness and what we see around us is alive and self-aware. This consciousness or aliveness is relative depending on the form it takes. For example, a human is more conscious and aware than a tree but nevertheless a tree is still conscious and self-aware.

So far, I've said that everything is made out of God stuff but now I would like to introduce another term that better describes the essence of what we see around us. **Everything is made out of divine consciousness or for short just consciousness.** Source is pure divine consciousness. So, if everything comes from source then it must be made of divine consciousness too.

This is a really important point, so let's have some examples. A potato is made of consciousness. A computer is made of consciousness. A gold nugget is made of consciousness. There is nothing in the game that is not made of divine consciousness.

Everything is consciousness. It's just that consciousness expresses itself in different ways. One of the ways consciousness expresses itself is as a human being.

We as human beings are like a drop of consciousness living in an ocean of consciousness.

This sentence above very simply but accurately describes our game. What it is saying is that not only are we human's conscious, we are also made of consciousness. So, there are two aspects to this. Firstly, there is the kind of consciousness that allows us to be alive and aware of the world around us. Secondly it is saying that consciousness is the building block of the game. Or in other words, everything is made from it including us.

A great analogy of this is an ocean wave you might see when standing on a beach. A wave is an expression of the ocean but it's not really a wave strictly speaking, it is still really the ocean. A wave is just something the ocean is doing for a very short time. In the same way, we as humans are an expression of consciousness. At our essence we are not really human, we are really consciousness. A human being is just something that consciousness is doing for about 80 years. 80 years is nothing in the grand scheme of things. It is a blink of an eye. The human being is just a temporary expression of consciousness just like a wave is a temporary expression of the ocean.

Another very similar analogy is that consciousness is like our hand and a human being is like a finger. The finger can't exist by itself and is really just part of the hand. In the same way a finger is just part of the hand, a human is just part of consciousness.

It is important to understand this relationship. Most people think they are a human being who has a life, or you could say is doing life. But we are flipping this on its head right here. You are not doing life, in fact life is doing you. **You are being lived by God**. It might seem strange to think of your life in this way but hopefully as you read on it will make more sense. Another analogy which points to the same place as this is the analogy of the dancer on a stage. Most people think they are the dancer (living life) and that the stage is the multiverse which is separate to them. This is not the way it works. You are life itself. You are the multiverse. You are actually the stage and the dancer is just an illusion.

These analogies may sound a little hard to fathom but as you read on this idea will be explained more so that you are very familiar with it. What it all seems to be pointing to is the idea that we aren't really this human being that we appear to be. **It is suggesting that the human being we think we are, is kind of like a temporary illusion, just like a wave which exists for a very short time.**

Oneness

Because we all came from that tiny but very dense divine consciousness at the big bang, it means that everything is one. Even though consciousness from the big bang has been scattered far and wide, it is still all one. This is because it was once all squashed together in a tiny but very dense singularity moments before it exploded outwards at the big bang. I have stated already that you are God. You are the God stuff or consciousness that has been spread far and wide. This God stuff or consciousness is all there is. Everything in this game is made out of it and came from it. Can you see what this means? It means that everything in existence is you. **You are the entire game or the entire multiverse.** This is the reason I said in the last section (the dancer analogy) that you are the stage. **You are more than just the human being you thought you were**. Much more it seems. You are everything and everything means everything.

When you look at the face of your loved ones, you are really looking at yourself. When you pick up your pet, you are really picking up yourself. When you tend to your garden, you are tending to yourself. You are one with everything. Every single thing in existence is you. Everything from stars to a blade of grass is you. You are even one with everyday objects. Even though many everyday objects have been manufactured in a factory. All the raw materials are divine consciousness. You are the entire universe or in other words the entire game. This is such a remarkable truth. For so long we believed we were just this one tiny human being and to find out that we are the entire game or the entire universe ...WOW! It can be summed up as follows:

You are God
God is everything
Everything is you

When people suddenly become spiritually enlightened, the first thing they usually do is laugh. They let go with a huge belly laugh. The reason they laugh is because they suddenly realise that they are the whole universe. The truth has finally hit home, they are everything that is. It is so funny to them that for so long they didn't know the truth. They actually thought they were just this one tiny little human. It seems so tiny and so far from the truth. They are laughing at how ridiculous the situation was. How could they have believed they were only one little human. When in fact, the whole time they were really everything in existence. This is the big cosmic joke. Talk about underestimating oneself.

In Chapter 4 Become Spiritually Enlightened; I will go into detail about what you can do to become enlightened. Hopefully you too, can become enlightened. Wouldn't it be great if you laughed out loud at the ridiculousness of the situation?

Consciousness is the fundamental reality of the game

There is a growing school of thought that consciousness is the only fundamental reality in the game.

For a long time, all physicists said that time and space known as spacetime was the fundamental reality of the game. By fundamental I mean that spacetime was considered to be the playing board upon which everything happens. But now more and more physicists believe that spacetime is an emergent property of consciousness. In other words, spacetime is something that comes out of the fundamental reality of consciousness. This means that it is consciousness that everything exists within. Consciousness is the playing board upon which everything happens. When you think about it, all human endeavours and achievements since the dawn of time have all occurred within consciousness. You cannot avoid consciousness. Nothing can be done outside of consciousness.

For example, Thomas Edison invented the light bulb. What an incredible invention that was at that time. Before then, everyone used candles for lighting. This invention was thought up and created within consciousness. The consciousness being Thomas Edison's mind. Every invention in our history has also been created using the consciousness of someone's mind. Yet, we rarely investigate what this actual consciousness is even though nothing in the history of the world exists outside of consciousness. Don't you think we should look into consciousness a little more? Instead of just accepting it is there. It is not just me as a growing number of scientists do believe that the only fundamental reality in the game is indeed consciousness.

What is consciousness though? How does it work? No one has any idea. Even though every person on the planet is conscious no one can explain it. If you want to make a physicist feel uncomfortable simply ask her to explain how consciousness works. It is a mystery. In science this is known as the "hard problem of consciousness." Specifically, what this hard problem of consciousness refers to is the problem of understanding how consciousness can arise from brain activity. No one has cracked this problem. There hasn't been any evidence at all showing how consciousness comes from brain activity. The reason they don't have any evidence at all is because consciousness does not come from brain activity, it's the fundamental reality of the universe. They are looking for something which doesn't exist.

Scientists say consciousness is caused by neurons firing in the brain, but they don't say how the firing neurons cause consciousness. They certainly cannot recreate it artificially. I would love to see someone invent or create an android that is fully conscious and can interact with the world. By interact I mean that this android could be truly self-aware; make decisions by itself, have morals, work, play, even socialise. It would be able to do everything that we can like ponder the meaning of life or share wistful anecdotes at a dinner-party. Can we do this? It's a big no. We can't, not even close. According to science we just need to create some neurons, get them to fire and put them inside a rag doll. Then the rag doll will come to life. The funny thing is we don't even know how to re-create a neuron let-alone bring a rag doll to life. I'm being light-hearted here but the point is we have no idea how to create a living, thinking being. Yet scientists tell us that consciousness has just emerged by itself over billions of years. They tell us that consciousness has occurred through natural selection and evolution.

It seems unlikely that something this complex can just occur naturally, almost by itself. It is more likely that it has happened by design. Starting way back at the big bang. Don't get me wrong. I do believe in evolution and natural selection. I just believe that the spark of consciousness that we and other lifeforms have comes from God. It is not just neurons that make a person conscious. It is a mystery, and I would add a miracle. We take life for granted when it is really the most extraordinary miracle.

Science states that human consciousness and thought all takes place in the brain, inside of the skull. However, this is not true as it has been proven from many researchers that human brain waves can be measured outside of the head. If thoughts can be detected 10 centimetres outside of your head, then they can exist 10 kilometres outside of your head or much further. Science tells us that every person walking around in the world has a little ball of consciousness existing inside of their skull. 8 billion balls of consciousness all interacting with each other. This is wrong. Everything is made out of consciousness not just brains. The entire game is consciousness itself and our brain is the thing we use to hook into this conscious and alive multiverse.

You could say the brain is similar to a radio. A radio when it is tuned correctly picks up radio signals. Our brain works the same way except it is tuned in to the divine consciousness which makes up the entire game. It picks up on signals of consciousness and translates them into thoughts. All thoughts exist out in the ether. We are unconsciously picking and choosing to have some of these thoughts. It all depends on the tuning of your brain. If you are positive and uplifted, then these are the kind of thoughts your brain will receive. If you are depressed and closed minded, you will receive thoughts that align with this state of mind.

This theory means that there is one giant mind. **The entire multiverse is that mind. Our brains are just a receiver which interacts with this one mind. Your brain is a consciousness interface.** We have already said that everything is made out of consciousness. This consciousness that everything is made up from is the one mind when seen collectively. We hook into this consciousness through our brain and that makes us conscious so that we can work, play and create.

When you tune your radio to a specific frequency you have many options available to yourself. You can tune in to everything from classical music to death metal music. These two types of music are very different, but you have the choice. In exactly the same way there are many different kinds of thoughts in the mind, and you have the ability to select any of these thoughts by using your brain. This is something that happens unconsciously and automatically. It is affected by things like your mood, your state of mind, your emotions and how evolved you are.

You are a soul made up of consciousness

It is clear now that you are the whole multiverse or the whole game but now I want to talk about this body you are. What is this human being you seem to be? All enlightened beings know they are much more than just a human being. They know they are consciousness itself (the whole multiverse or the whole game) but what then is this human being and how does this fit in to the picture. The answer is that **each human being is a soul made out of divine consciousness from source.** You are both everything there is, and you are also experiencing life localised as a divine **soul** within a human being.

We are starting to get a picture of how life works. **We are a divine soul playing an extraordinary game.** We call this extraordinary game life. I said earlier that you are everything in the multiverse and now I am saying you are a divine soul. You might think this is contradictory but it's not. You can look at yourself in two ways. You are both everything in the entire game and also a single soul that is localised in a body. **The single soul is one with everything in the game and that's how you are both a soul and the entire multiverse, because of the oneness of everything.**

In Chapter 3 We Are Living in a Computer Simulation; we will go very deep into describing how this game for the ages operates and it is truly mind blowing. For now, we will continue to investigate this idea of us being pure consciousness in the form of a soul who came to Earth deliberately to live out some specific experiences for source.

The veil of forgetting

You may be wondering why you don't remember anything from before this game you are now playing. You don't remember because you are not supposed too. When your soul incarnated on Earth you agreed to a process known as the veil of forgetting. This process wiped from your memory all knowledge of your time in the spirit world before this incarnation. Almost every soul that incarnates on Earth undergoes the veil of forgetting. This ensures that each soul experiences this game very deeply. That it feels very real. This is what source wants. He wants to experience every possible situation and emotion as deeply as possible. **The whole point of the game is to play it and then get to the point where you remember you are a divine soul. Once you remember the truth you can work on transcending the belief you are a person and continue playing the game with the firm knowledge and belief that you are God. This is enlightenment and this book will tell you how to do this.**

For many people reading this book right now, this is a seminal moment. You may have lived hundreds or thousands of lifetimes and have been totally under the power of the veil of forgetting the entire time. But right now, might be the first time that this veil has been pulled back ever so slightly revealing the truth to you.

The truth that you are not a human being but actually a divine soul playing a game that you planned out in the spirit world before deliberately incarnating here on Earth. What a magnificent moment that is! For the first time you may have a better perspective on this thing we call life which is really a game.

In Chapter 5 The Meaning of Life; we will build on this and fully explain the purpose of life.

Incarnating into the game

You have most likely had hundreds if not thousands of incarnations. Reincarnation as taught by many eastern religions is a truth of the game.

It is a progression. You start off at a low level and usually progress higher with each incarnation. For example, you may have been a dog in one game and then the next game you might have been human for the first time. Then the game after that you might be a human again but this time with a completely different set of circumstances and experiences. It keeps going higher and of course you are not limited to Earth. You can incarnate on any habitable planet in the game.

If you decide to incarnate on Earth, two of the biggest decisions you will have to make are what country will you be born in and who your parents will be. You pick the country and parents who are most suitable for the life you have planned. It is not just random. You choose them out of billions of options.

You also choose your body with the same rationale. The body that is most suitable for this lifetime. Many people dislike their body. They wish they had a different body. It's important to love your body and be grateful for your body. Use this knowledge that you specifically chose this body you are in right now to learn how to love it. After all it is tailor made for you.

Each soul has their own specific developmental goals to work towards. For example, one soul may have a goal of developing higher levels of trust. So, this soul may incarnate as a vision impaired person so that they can learn to trust a guide dog or human helpers. Another soul may desire to learn about abundance. This soul may choose parents in a poor country who themselves are very poor. It is all set up to give the soul an opportunity to overcome their life circumstances. To learn how to feel and create abundance; be it money, health or whatever it is that they desire from life.

You have heard the expression "old soul." Old souls have had more incarnations than most. However just because one soul has had more incarnations than another does not make that soul better. They are simply at a different stage of the game. At some point every soul successfully gets to the end of the game. It's impossible not too, so relax there is no pressure.

Now for an important clarification. From a pure non-dual perspective there isn't a soul hopping from body to body like a traveller with a passport. When I say one soul incarnates many times, I'm not talking literally. It's just a way of pointing to oneness. The word "soul" is just there so the mind can make sense of it. So in this book I make a concession and don't teach the highest truth, instead I talk about souls so that it is much easier to understand. What we call reincarnation is really just consciousness showing up as different lives. In the highest truth, nobody comes back at all. Life just keeps appearing in different ways. This is all happening outside of time. It's happening all at the same time, which is right now.

Time is an illusion

Time as we know it, is not real. It is an illusion.

The great physicist Albert Einstein once wrote "People like us who believe in physics know that the distinction between past, present and future is only a stubbornly persistent illusion." Einstein was able to see through the illusion of time. He knew all was not as it seemed. His brilliance told him something was just not quite right about time. Whether he knew this from his own intuition or from his mathematical equations, I'm not sure, but he was on point.

Einstein was the first person to realise that space and time go hand and hand. He called the phenomena spacetime. He explained in his theory of special relativity that the experience of the flow of time is relative to the observer and their situation. So, time is personal. If you move, time slows down for you. For example, let's say you were on-board a rocket that went right around the sun at high speed and came back to Earth. Travelling at that high-speed, time will have slowed down for you but not for everyone else back on Earth. So, when you get back to Earth you would have time travelled into the future. This time travel would only be very small but if you were to travel further and faster (like near the speed of light) the time travel would be much more significant. Travelling for 5 years in a spaceship at 99% of the speed of light corresponds to roughly 36 years passing on Earth. So, by the time you got back after 5 years, you would have time travelled 31 years into the future. This is all very interesting, but we still don't know what time really is.

The truth is that no one, not even physicists, know what time is. Time is necessary so that we can deeply experience all the events in our life. Some physicists believe time to be the 4th dimension. The following is a definition of time many physicists use. "Time is the process that brings the unknown future into the recorded past, via the present." This is a very linear way of looking at time. The present and future events are treated as quantum events. This means, they are unknowable and based on probability. Whilst the past is knowable, so it is akin to classical physics. This is not how we will be treating time. The view of this book is that time is an illusion, but it allows the game to work properly so it is a necessary illusion. This is in keeping with what Einstein had to say on the topic of time. We will base our understanding as follows. **Everything that has ever happened or ever will happen, is happening right now**.

This is hard for us to imagine as our brains find this concept difficult, but it is the most accurate way of thinking about time. This concept of time also means that something you do in the future can affect the past. This is known as retro-causality. That is a head scratcher. We know very well that the past affects the future. There is no problem understanding that. But the opposite is also true. Something in the future from our perspective could affect something that's already seemed to have happened in the past. Again, the best way to understand this, is knowing that time is not real and that in actuality everything is happening all at the same time, which is right now.

In the spirit world time does not exist like it does here. An entire lifetime on Earth only takes up a few moments in the spirit world. This is extraordinary but true. When your body dies, and your soul returns to the spirit world you will soon start to forget much of this life. It's like when we wake from a vivid dream at night. In the morning we can remember the dream quite clearly, but it starts to fade after a while. This is what will happen when your body dies, and your soul returns home to the spirit world. Your soul will first conduct a life review where it goes over the life it has just lived. It will review the lessons learned, areas of growth achieved and areas still to be worked on. After the life review there is no point hanging on to this life, so the memories start to fade, and your soul moves on.

The fact that your entire life only takes a few moments in the spirit world may sound disturbing but it's really freeing. We don't need to take life so seriously. We can just enjoy life knowing it really is just a game. Think of it this way. We are immortal. We live forever. So, this life is really just like a blink of an eye. In the grand scheme of our immortal life, this game is a very tiny part of it. So, relax and chill out! With this perspective we don't need to worry so much. We don't need to be so hard on ourselves. This is just a game we are playing here and its over in a flash.

Consider this analogy; say you play a computer game one evening. The next day are you still worried or even caring about how you performed in the game? Of course not. It is just not that important. You have probably forgotten all about it. It's the same with this game we are playing here on Earth. It too is a game and once it's over our soul does not need to remember it forever.

So, we just don't need to fret so much. Playing this game is meant to be fun and joyful. It's usually not fun for most people because they take life and themselves so seriously. Imagine how much better the world would be if everyone knew that this life is just a game and that they have a home in the spirit world for eternity. Everyone would breathe a huge sigh of relief. This knowledge is really important because it does change everything. It creates a different perspective on life. It can be summed up in three words; "**Nothing really matters.**"

What is Heaven like?

Let's now take a close look at what goes on in the spirit world. The spirit world is our home. It is important to realise that Earth is not our home and that when our body dies our soul will return home. We have been using the term spirit world but there are many other names that it is known as. Christian religions call it Heaven. Sometimes it is called the other side.

To know what heaven is like, we can look at what people have said who have had a near death experience. There are many people who have died for a short period of time and crossed over to the other side and their stories are remarkedly similar. I will be drawing here on what these people have said.

When people have had near death experiences, they very often report seeing a tunnel of light. When they walk through the tunnel, they say they appear in a beautiful natural setting. It seems that the settings in Heaven are akin to the most stunning scenery that we have here on Earth, except it's even more magnificent. Perhaps every blade of grass is perfect and every flower at its most radiant. When a soul first comes out of the tunnel into this natural setting they will still be appearing in their human form. This form is only temporary. They are met by family and friends who have also passed. The reason for this is because the soul that has just died is still associating with their just completed life on Earth, so seeing their past relatives is a beautiful moment.

The soul will not stay in their human form however. Those relatives who appeared in their human form were only doing this temporarily to comfort the newly returning soul. Once back in heaven every newly returning soul re-joins with its higher self. This is the form that each soul will exhibit in heaven, that of the higher self. The higher self is also sometimes called the "real self" and this is who you really are. I will explain more about the higher self later in this chapter.

Soon after returning home a game review will take place. Some sources say you do this review yourself while other people who have had a near death experience say other spiritual elders assist in the review. There is agreement in the spiritual community however that there is absolutely no one judging you on your game, like many religions say there is. Any spiritual elders who assist in the review are not there to cast judgement. They are there to help you in this process. They are fully supportive of the soul the whole way. The soul can see every moment of their game at will and they see every moment from every perspective too. This means that if you hurt an ex-partner for example, you will see this hurt from the perspective of the ex-partner. This review is very thorough, and it will highlight what growth has taken place and what areas still need work.

In the spirit world each soul is a member of what we call a soul group. This is kind of like your family in Heaven. Members of a soul group usually incarnate together. In one game your brothers and sisters may be from your soul group. In another game these same souls may be your life partner and friends. Even animal souls reside in the spirit world and are part of your soul group. Before incarnating you make contracts with members of your soul group. You plan everything out with each other.

For example, you might have a contract to hurt a second soul in an incarnation by doing something to them on Earth which causes hurt. The second soul wants this to happen to them. This could be for karmic reasons or just because it wants to experience this situation. The second soul may have agreed that its part of the contract is to forgive the first soul for the hurt it received.

Each soul will incarnate as both male or female depending on which game it is. Many souls may have a bias towards one gender. For example, a soul might want to experience femininity more than masculinity. It will still sometimes incarnate as a male but just not as often as it does as a female. Experiencing and exploring masculinity and femininity is something many souls put a focus on. Quite often souls who want to deeply explore one side of these two opposites may decide to incarnate as something different from being a heterosexual.

Life in Heaven is blissful. Not just because of the setting but because emotionally you will only experience happiness, joy, peace and the full spectrum of positive emotions. There are no challenges, difficulties and suffering like we encounter here on Earth. It is paradise. Have you ever wondered what happens in Heaven? The cliché is sitting on a cloud whilst playing a harp. It is not really like that although you could do that if you wanted to. It is my belief from the research I've done that you can do anything you like in Heaven. You can conjure up any scenario you wish, kind of like the holo-deck in the Star Trek series. This means any possible experience you could ever think of can be had instantly and for as long as you wish. Creation of anything you want is instant and communication with other souls is telepathic.

You may be surprised to learn that there are incredible libraries and amazing schools that you can go to in Heaven to learn. Just because you are in heaven it doesn't mean you don't learn anymore. Yes, life on Earth is like a school and souls learn lessons here but they do in Heaven too. The distinction is that lessons in Heaven are theoretical while lessons on Earth are practical and perhaps much more revelatory. You learn much more and more profoundly here on Earth. I am sure there is much more that happens in Heaven but because we cannot remember anything from before this incarnation we will have to wait until we go home again to find out.

As mentioned earlier there is no place called hell in the afterlife. It does not exist. Hell is here on Earth because Earth is the place where people hurt each other.

The game is a place of learning and Earth is one of the most difficult incarnations there is. I will explain more about how Earth compares to other planets in the game, in Chapter 5 The Meaning of Life; but as a spoiler this life on Earth is considered so difficult and painful that only the most courageous souls are prepared to incarnate here.

Life in other parts of the game

When a soul decides to incarnate into the game it can decide exactly where it wants to go. It will choose which planet it wants to incarnate on. There most certainly is intelligent life on planets other than Earth. There is a way we can classify planets based on how highly evolved the life forms are on each planet. I will also explain this fully in Chapter 5: The Meaning of Life.

There are many planets which are home to very highly evolved beings. We on Earth wonder why we have not been visited by beings from other worlds but who is to say this hasn't happened? The great spiritual teacher Aaron Abke has said "Do we expect them to land their ships on the White House lawn." Of course not. We are simply not ready yet for such an event. Such an event is sometimes referred to as "declaration." Perhaps when we have evolved much further and stopped warring with each other, they may make themselves more known and a declaration might happen.

Earth has a particular place in the galactic community. It is a $3^{rd}/4^{th}$ density planet. I will explain what this means in Chapter 5: The Meaning of Life - the seven densities of life. For now, I will just say that we have our place, and that the galactic community has **a no interference policy**. We must evolve and work out our problems ourselves. This is why no alien ships have landed on the White House lawn because they are not allowed to until we are ready.

There will come a time when we are ready for a declaration by the galactic community. Before this happens, we as a world must know the basics of who we really are, and we must have overcome the limitations of living as an ego (seeing ourselves and each other as being distinct and separate individuals). In other words, we will need to know the truth. Once it becomes common knowledge that we are all one and that one thing is God simply experiencing life as a human being for a while; when this and other spirituality basics are taught in school to our children then a declaration may happen. At the moment we don't even know the basics of how life works, and we don't understand anything about how the galactic community operates. If, and when a declaration happens, it will shake the foundations of the world's religions. Can you imagine what the Catholic Church for example, may have to say to its flock if we were to be visited by a spaceship full of highly evolved beings. They will have to come up with something because this would be an event of seismic and biblical change. It is not a question of if this happens, it is more a question of when.

Highly evolved beings will not land on the White House lawn, but they do visit in a clandestine manner. They are careful to not reveal themselves on mass but in the far past they were more prepared to do this. They have in the past helped us progress forward. It is believed by many people including myself, that highly evolved beings helped us in the past construct healing centres which helped raise our collective vibration. I am referring to the pyramids in Egypt and to places like Stonehenge in England.

The United States Department of Defence are well aware of UFO's. They don't use that abbreviation, instead they call alien ships UAP's (Unidentified Aerial Phenomena). In August 2020, the Department of Defence set up a taskforce called the UAP taskforce. The purpose of this taskforce was the study of unidentified flying objects. This taskforce was set up after repeated sightings by pilots flying off the Atlantic Coast. One pilot who appeared on a 60 Minutes TV episode said he saw UFO's on a daily basis for two years. It was sightings like these that finally made people at the US Department of Defence take notice. This UAP taskforce has now been succeeded by a new group called AOIMSG (Airborne Object Identification and Management Synchronisation Group).

All this is evidence that other intelligent life exists in the multiverse. The most important thing I wish to say about beings from other parts of the game is that they are God too. Or more precisely they too are divine souls made out of consciousness, just like we are.

It is naïve to think that a soul will just want to incarnate on Earth. Remember we believe there could be 10,000,000,000,000,000,000,000,000 planets in our observable universe. That is just what we can see with our telescopes. There is plenty of scope for souls to look elsewhere to live rather than just Earth. All souls, from all planets, reside in the spirit world between lives. Heaven is their home as well.

Karma- The law of cause and effect

We have already looked at the spiritual truth that is reincarnation. Another truth of the game which is taught by many religions is the law of karma. Also known as the law of cause and effect.

It means that whatever energy or actions we put out, we get back, good or bad. It's the concept of reap what you sow. So, if you go about your life ripping people off for example, then expect to be ripped off yourself. If it doesn't happen this life, it will in the next. Of course, karma can also be considered good. An example of this may be a person who genuinely appreciates others and always takes time to personally thank them and give praise when she can. This person will have this come back to her. She will most likely be appreciated by others in her life and will receive the same feedback. If it doesn't happen for her in this life, then it will in her coming incarnations.

I was living in Melbourne Australia around 2010, when I had to stop full time work as a teacher due to a health concern. I didn't know it at the time, but I had a chronic disease called fibromyalgia. This condition causes pain in the body. This obviously put some financial pressure on myself and my wife. I had been unemployed for a few months as there weren't many jobs, I thought I could do with this health issue. However, I did see a flyer in the window of the local library, asking for volunteers for what was called a homework club for school kids. It was only two hours a week, so I volunteered.

All I had to do was to help these kids do their homework after school in the library. I helped out and I really enjoyed it. It wasn't difficult work and I loved teaching, so it was a lot better than being at home doing nothing.

I had been doing this job for only another 2 months when out of the blue I was offered a casual teaching position. The job was to teach students who were in a special setting some of which were currently in a juvenile prison. It sounded like a tough job, but the great thing about it was the fact that it was team teaching, and the class sizes were very small.

This was totally unexpected, and I would never have normally thought to do such a job. It was not going to be as taxing as a regular teaching job where there is just one teacher for 25 plus kids. It was perfect. So, I took it. I do believe it was karma that got me this new teaching job. Had I not helped out at the homework club, I really don't think this job would have landed in my lap. I only did this job for a short time, but I really valued the experience. I do believe that whenever we are of service in any way the game changes. New opportunities come up. Literally, new, and different realities emerge that simply weren't there before.

Here is another example of Karma. Zola was a lady living in Africa who had a huge vegetable garden as well as numerous fruit trees. She was one of the most generous people you could come across. Over the years she gave away to friends and family much of the produce from her garden. She would gift bananas, watermelon, mangoes as well as sweet potato, cucumbers and peppers. Her friends and family gratefully received her gifts. Zola had an abundance mind set. She didn't fear that she would not have enough for herself. In other words, she didn't have a scarcity mindset. The universe rewarded Zola for her generosity. Year after year her garden become more and more plentiful. It gave forth much more produce than she needed for herself. Her fruit trees without fail every year were full of fruit with no disease at all. The same with her vegetable garden. It was incredibly plentiful. The soil in which this produce grew remained fertile and rich in nutrients. The garden always seemed to get just enough rain. This is a great example of how the universe can give back to someone who has put out.

The law of attraction

We have the ability to attract into our lives whatever it is that we desire. This power we have is known as the law of attraction. This law was popularised by the excellent movie and book known as "The Secret" by Rhonda Byrne.

There is a term that is often used to describe this process. It is manifestation. The ability to manifest whatever it is you want is a law of the game. It is a fully-fledged law, just as true as say, the law of gravity.

If you are a positive person with positive thoughts and you combine this with positive actions and upbeat positive emotions, then you can expect that you will manifest positive outcomes in your life. This is just the way the game works. If on the other hand you are a negative person always fearing the worst and you combine this with negative emotions and you don't take positive actions, then I am afraid you will get negative outcomes. This is not a matter of one person having better luck than another, it is just a basic law of the universe. Basically, you get what you expect in life. Life is kind of like a mirror. It shows you whatever it is that you are putting out. We are not just victims of fate. We are creators. We co-create our life with source.

We co-create our life with source through thoughts, emotions, and actions.

This trio of things determines the results we get in our life. So, it is really important for people to realise they are at cause rather than at affect. By this I mean people are not just passive participants in life getting a mixture of results from just random luck. No, they are in the driver's seat co-creating their life. It means that you are responsible for everything that has happened in your life. You are not a victim. You can't blame anyone else when you know you are a co-creator. You have manifested everything in your life and you will continue to do so whether you know it or not.

This process is happening all the time. We are subconsciously co-creating our lives through thought, emotions, and actions. If we want to, we can consciously try to manifest something specific using our conscious mind. Let's give an example of Alice who wants to manifest a vacation to the Greek Islands. For her, this is a vacation of a lifetime. To manifest this using the law of attraction, Alice would need to follow the following steps:

1. Imagine in her mind having whatever it is right now. She must not imagine the process of getting it, just imagine having the final result right at this moment. (So, Alice imagines she is right now lying on the beach in Mykonos, looking out to sea while sipping a cocktail).

2. Fully feel the feelings that come with having this object or experience. Turn up the feelings as much as possible. For example, if it's a feeling of gratitude, then feel as much gratitude as you can and hold that feeling of gratitude for at least a minute. (So, Alice feels as much gratitude as she can as she imagines lying on the beach sipping a cocktail. She also imagines the taste of the cocktail).

3. Keep doing steps one and two multiple times each day. Do both steps before you go to sleep at night while you are lying in bed. This is because you are implanting it into the subconscious mind just before the subconscious mind activates when you enter the dream state.

4. Take some actions which are congruent with whatever it is you want to manifest. (So, Alice starts researching the Greek Islands on the internet. She watches YouTube videos on the Greek Islands. She buys a travel guide on Greece).

5. Wait and allow time to pass. Stay open for any unexpected turn of events. **The law of attraction has a time lag** so there is usually a waiting period before you get what you want.

You do have the ability to manifest anything you desire. **The key thing is belief.** You must believe you will get it. We can fool ourselves sometimes, but the game knows whether or not we do believe deep down. If we don't believe we will not manifest it. So, in the example above Alice must truly believe a vacation in Greece is going to happen. To be more precise she must believe it has already happened. That is the key as you do steps 1 and 2. Believing, truly **believing it has already happened.**

We are using our minds to manifest using the law of attraction. We use both the conscious mind and the subconscious mind. If the subconscious mind is not congruent with the conscious mind it can be harder to manifest what you want. So, in the example above, if Alice harbours any limiting beliefs in her subconscious mind, she will find it may take longer to make it happen. It is possible that Alice believes in her subconscious mind that; (i) she does not deserve a vacation like this. Maybe she believes; (ii) it will just be too expensive, and she won't be able to raise the funds. These are limiting beliefs stored in the subconscious and they can easily derail successfully manifesting something big like this.

There are mental processes we can perform on ourselves to clear away these types of limiting beliefs. In the appendix at the back of the book, I have written out instructions for a powerful process which removes these types of limiting beliefs from the subconscious mind and can be done in one minute.

With this example of Alice, she possibly has two limiting beliefs to get rid of. This type of work does require you to be self-aware, so that you know what might be going on in your subconscious mind. You have to be able to ascertain what unconscious beliefs may be holding you back.

Another example is a man looking for love who is wanting to use the law of attraction to find a life partner. He will need to use his judgement to look into his subconscious and ascertain if any unconscious blocks may be hiding there. With relationships there are some very common limiting beliefs that many people harbour. Here are a few typical ones:

I don't deserve a partner.
I am not good enough to have a partner.
No-one out there will like me.

These types of subconscious limiting beliefs can be erased with the process at the end of this book.

The best results using the law of attraction are when your soul is onboard with your mind. You use the mind to manifest but if the soul has other ideas, it will be harder to manifest.

It could be for Alice that her soul does indeed want Alice to travel. Travel opens up the mind and expands one's horizons. So, with her soul on board it is more likely that the universe will somehow get Alice on to that beach in Mykonos.

This is part of the fun with the law of attraction; seeing how the universe delivers what you want. Never worry about how it's going to happen. Leave that up to the game. Just concentrate on the end result, because who knows how it might come about and remember the key thing is believing it's already happened.

When people first have a spiritual awakening, it is often the law of attraction that appeals to them. They love the idea of manifesting whatever it is that they want. It must be known however that using the law of attraction alone does not bring long term peace and happiness. It is a useful tool to use but it is not the main game. The main game is spiritual enlightenment and lifelong happiness. This is what this book is concerned with. The law of attraction is great in that it attracts people to spirituality initially but eventually people are going to find that even if they are successfully manifesting many things in their life, they are still not happy and they are still experiencing some emotional suffering.

The purpose of the law of attraction is to speed up your evolution and get you closer to becoming enlightened. Achieving all your desires through the law of attraction but still not being truly happy is a powerful way to finally accept that the real salvation is in realising that you are God. At the beginning of most people's spiritual journey, realising that the person you seem to be doesn't exist is not that appealing to seekers. The spiritual seeker needs to be ready for this. Law of attraction teachings speed up a soul's evolution so that they can get ready faster. It is not that you can't co-create your life because you can. You have been doing it your whole life whether you knew it or not. It is more that you don't need to put so much emphasis on it as it is better to just let life unfold and enjoy the game. You can never attain peace through law of attraction anyway. You can only achieve peace and happiness by realising you are a soul and not the individual person you thought you were.

I mentioned above it is better to just let life unfold. Sure, you can consciously manifest something using the law of attraction from time to time, but you don't need to because you don't know what is best for you. The universe does. It is better to just feel good and let the universe bring you surprises. Remember you co-create with your thoughts, emotions and actions. Here is a tip for you. Adopt this belief:

The universe is conspiring for my success

Adopt this belief and adopt positive upbeat emotions like excitement and curiosity and let the universe surprise you with wonderful things. This is better than trying to consciously control the manifestation process. I adopted this belief myself after attending a Christopher Howard personal development seminar. It has worked for me better than I could have ever imagined. The game just keeps giving me incredible outcomes. Even when I think I have made a mistake the game will give me some incredible silver lining. I highly recommend adopting this belief as it is so powerful. **Remember you just need to believe it and it will be true**. I know that no matter what situation I am in that the universe is secretly conspiring for my success!

Every soul has an agenda

Your soul has an agenda for this current game you are playing now. In other words, your soul has some specific things it wants you to experience in this game. Your soul's agenda for your game right now is probably quite different to the agenda that exists in your mind. There is a reason for this.

Your soul looks at your game from a much higher perspective than you see from. For example, you may be really wanting to get a promotion at work. Or maybe you just really want to earn more money somehow. This is what you want, but it may not be what your soul wants. From your soul's perspective earning more money may just not be that important. Your soul may wish for you to pay back some karma from a previous game for one thing. That could be the reason why you have been treated badly recently. Then it may be wanting you to learn some specific lessons, like learning how to forgive or learning how to be more empathetic.

Can you see how your soul may have a completely different agenda for your life than the one that exists in your mind? Your soul may be neutral to the idea of you having more money. So, it's possible you could still manifest that. It's just that the soul is not as focused on that as your mind is.

Great happiness in life can be found by aligning your wishes from this life with what you believe is your soul's agenda. If you are perceptive enough to suspect what your soul's agenda is, then you can embrace these things and go after them. In this way you align with your soul's agenda. When this happens, the game goes smoothly. This is when the magic happens. You are not fighting or resisting your soul's agenda. When you resist, this is when you experience a lot of emotional suffering in life.

I remember around 2010 I was staying in a motel whilst away for a weekend break. I came across a flyer for a personal development seminar. It was called at the time "Break Through to Success." The main speaker was a man called Chris Howard. Normally I would not be interested in something like this but for some reason I had a strong intuition that the universe really wanted me to attend this seminar.

In a nutshell, I attended this seminar, and I loved every minute of it. It really spoke to me at the time. The main focus of the teachings was about taking responsibility for your life. Not being a victim. Leading a bigger life with bigger goals. Living with authenticity and integrity. It is not an exaggeration to say this course changed my life. I gave my all during this weekend seminar. This is an example of my personal desire to improve and develop myself aligning 100% with my soul's agenda. With my mind and soul 100% focused on giving my all at this seminar I walked out at the end of it as a completely different person. I felt like I had undergone a transformation. I felt like I was somehow a better version of myself.

How do you know what it is your soul is wanting from you? To know what your soul's agenda is, sometimes you need to use your intuition. You may just have a knowing.

You can also know your soul's agenda by looking at some patterns that have been playing out in your life. For example, maybe you have had a few romantic partners leave you or cheat on you. Why does this keep happening? It could be this is karma from another game you have played. Another reason could be that your soul wants to know what it's like to be betrayed. Maybe your soul wants to know what it's like to forgive those partners that hurt you too.

In this way you can look for patterns from your past and use intuition to align with your soul's agenda. In this example you could work on completely forgiving your ex-partners. Holding absolutely no grudge, no malice. Then concentrate on a new relationship, letting go of the past. When we align the way we live, with our soul's agenda, everything just makes more sense. It is a far better way to live.

You have angels and spirit guides with you all the time

So, are you on your own in this game or is there some divine help? The answer is a resounding yes! Yes, you have a lot of help that most people don't even know about.

Firstly, every single soul on Earth always has a guardian angel and multiple spirit guides with them. They don't usually make themselves visible, but they are indeed with you, including right now. Their role is to help you in this game. They will help keep you safe and help you achieve your soul's agenda.

They will literally intervene in your life to help if needed. They try to communicate with you by creating synchronicities. Synchronicities are those seeming coincidences that occur in your life. There is a common saying "There is no such thing as a coincidence, everything happens for a reason." Indeed, this is true. Many times, synchronicities are your spirit guides or angels trying to give you a message to help you.

The trick is to look out for synchronicities in your life and use your intuition to interpret what the message might be. For example, let's say you are a gambler, and you are about to use your credit card to fund your online casino account. You have some problems getting the deposit to go through as the wi-fi is playing up. You have been trying to make this deposit for a few minutes. Do you just keep trying? The answer could be no, give up. This could very well be your guides trying to send you a message, "Stop, don't gamble. You are going to lose." This is a really obvious example. Sometimes the messages from your spirit guides and angels will be subtle.

The more aware of synchronicities you become the more you will receive and your angels and guides will give you more and more complex and elaborate signs. In this way the more aware you become the more help you will receive. The common denominator in most synchronicities is that they usually involve seeming co-incidences and they convey information to you that can help you in your life.

Your angels and spirit guides are with you all the time but a lot of the time they are twiddling their divine thumbs. They don't have much to do, because you don't realise they are with you. You have not been picking up on their synchronicities. They can help you in so many ways. Sometimes they can send you messages in the form of you overhearing a snippet of someone else's conversation or an ad on TV might be giving you something to think about. It can come in many different ways. Sometimes your phone may ring at just the vital moment. There are countless ways synchronicities can come. The key thing is to look out for them and use your intuition to know whether there is a message for you or not.

Talk to your angels and spirit guides! You can ask them for help when you need it. They want to help you, but you need to ask. I remember one time I was travelling to Mumbai, India from Melbourne, Australia. It was just after the horrific Mumbai bombings. I was going through the security check and bag check at Mumbai International Airport. It was very heavily guarded and there were lots of police officers with assault rifles. The atmosphere was dark and serious. They were checking every bag very closely. It was a stressful situation. I remember asking my spirit guides to help me get through quickly and safely. I had some important homeopathic medicines for myself that I needed to get through without being x-rayed so I asked my spirit guides to make sure the medicines would not be scanned and in the end, they weren't. This is just one example. Don't hesitate to ask for help because your angels and spirit guides do want to help you.

Your angels and spirit guides are helping you in your game. They are working behind the scenes to manipulate reality for your benefit. They have control over matter as well as space and time. They know what is best for your spiritual growth and they do intervene in your game to give you the experiences and results you need.

Everything happens for a good reason

Nothing in the game happens by mistake. As previously mentioned, everything happens for a reason. I prefer to say everything happens for a good reason. Sometimes you just have to look at the very big picture to see the good but it's always there. Often that good thing is a valuable life lesson. It may even be a lesson needed for a future game.

If you could see just how perfect your life is, you would be amazed. Everything comes together just so, at just the right time. No matter how seemingly big or small those things are. What is happening in this game is the unfolding of the life plan you put in place before incarnating here on Earth. You knew in advance exactly what was going to happen.

Your destiny is already assured. Remember time is an illusion. Your destiny is happening right now, and you can't help but achieve it.

It is really freeing when you take this onboard. You don't need to beat yourself up over any mistakes you think you have made. You can let go of past regrets by just realising that those things were meant to happen all along. They were all part of the plan. Your plan. Your divine plan!

This doesn't mean you can just be a passive participant in the game. No, you are here to play the game. You are co-creating the game with source. Get out and about and co-create holding that knowledge in your mind that everything in the game is unfolding just as it should. You may desire something but there are no guarantees that you will get it. You may do your best to manifest it and it still might not happen. That may be because you are not meant to have this thing or experience right now. Source has other ideas for you. I once heard a very wise person say that when you pray to source and ask for something in the game you will only get one of three possible answers from source. Those are; (i) yes, (ii) soon, (iii) I have something better in mind.

Do we have free will?

This is a question which has been debated by philosophers for centuries. Are we in control or is everything mapped out? Most spiritual teachers teach that free will is an illusion. For a long time, I struggled with this idea that I am not in control of my destiny. However, over time I too have concluded that we do not have free will like it appears we do. This can seem unsettling. We want to believe that we have the freedom to do whatever it is we want to do.

The truth is that the person we think we are, is not real. There is no person making decisions. It just seems that there is. I will deeply explore this concept later in this book. This idea in spirituality is that there is no "do-er" of things. Until now you thought you were a person who does stuff. What I am saying here is that this is wrong and that in fact there is no do-er who does anything. If there is no do-er making decisions then what the heck is going on? How does stuff actually happen? The answer is incredibly simple. Everything is just happening. **Life happens by itself**. Yes that is correct. **Life simply unfolds by itself.** Everything is pre-determined. Everything you do and every experience you have was written down in the spirit world. You knew every single thing that was going to happen to you in the game when you were still in the spirit world about to incarnate. You knew every event, every movement, every scratch of your face. You have no control over this and you can't change or avoid destiny. **Life occurs by itself.**

This idea although so seemingly disturbing is incredibly freeing. It links with the previous section which explains that everything happens perfectly and for a good reason. It is freeing because if everything is simply happening by itself and you have no free will then you don't need to feel guilty about anything that has happened in your past. How can you feel guilty about something which happened by itself without your free will being involved? It makes no sense to feel guilty because you never had any control over the situation.

Many of us ruminate over things we have done in the past. Mistakes we think we have made. What I am saying here is that you don't need to beat yourself up over these things. You didn't make that mistake because there is no you. What happened was meant to happen. It was simply part of destiny unfolding. So, give yourself a break.

Think about my favourite movie; "Star Wars". The story was already written before they started filming. Luke Sky Walker was already destined to meet Yoda. Always going to face Darth Vader and eventually save the entire galaxy. Luke didn't make this happen, he just went along for the ride. That is no-doership (it means life is happening through you not because of you). Real life is exactly the same. Just like any movie your life has already been scripted and there is nothing you can do to break out of that script.

Let's have a playful example. Imagine a little girl who is told by her parents about no-doership. She thinks to herself "I am going to trick God! I am going to do something really random that God didn't put in the script for my life". So what she does is perform a headstand against her bedroom wall. Upside down she sings the lyrics to her favourite song. She stands up and claps nine times. Jumps seven times. Does a cartwheel. Repeats her name five times, each time with a funny voice. "I tricked you", she says to the Universe! You didn't expect that did you? She thinks to herself.

Of course God already knew. Every headstand, every song, every clap, every jump and every funny voice. She thinks she is tricking the universe, but really, she is just having the most wildly fun time through the script life had already written. The upshot of this is simple. **You can't go rouge in life no matter how hard you try.** Is this not amazing? It's a life changing shift in perspective. This frees you from remorse and guilt. Everything that happened was meant to happen.

This concept has the backing from a very interesting experiment which tested this theory of no-doership. In an experiment participants sat in front of a button and were told to decide whether to push it with either their left or right hand. They were free to make this decision whenever they wanted to but they had to remember at which time they felt they had made up their mind. The researchers were able to predict by looking at brain signals which hand the participants were going to use a whole **seven seconds** before the participants themselves had conscious awareness of their decision. Yes, they knew what hand the participant was going to use seven seconds before the participants themselves knew. So, what is going on here? **Is life from our perspective on a seven second delay?** How could they know in advance? What we do know is that the participants were destined to choose one particular hand and that the experience of choosing was an illusion albeit a very convincing one. It is fascinating and it certainly gives us some pause for thought. Every single one of our daily decisions are illusory and in actual fact everything is set in stone.

Physicists working with quantum mechanics have found that when they go deep into the math of the universe, there is no need for causality to be factored into the equations. By causality I mean the usual cause and effect that we see in our lives. An example of cause and effect is if I hit a pool ball with a cue it will roll over the pool table into other pool balls. It seems that the math at this level works better if we leave causality out completely. Cause and effect are linked to free will yet the math that describes our universe has no need for it at all.

What all this means is that the idea there is a person who is in control making free will decisions is wrong. Before you incarnated onto this Earth you wrote the script for the life you were about to live. You knew exactly what was about to happen in your life before it had even started, and the game is simply playing out. Destiny is unfolding. As it says in the spiritual text; A course in miracles, "It is written." You cannot help but fulfil your destiny and this knowledge alone is comforting. Everything is happening just as it should. This game is playing out perfectly so enjoy the ride.

This doesn't mean that you should just be passive and not make decisions and not act in this game. This is one of the game's paradoxes. Making positive decisions and developing yourself is always good. Living with integrity and doing good in the world is rewarding and always worthwhile. Every time you do good in the world your soul is evolving even though there is no free will. By being kind you are evolving. By being selfless you are evolving. By being empathetic you are evolving. This is the key point. It seems counter intuitive but that's the way the game works.

Everything I have written above about no free will is from the perspective of the individual ego or person. What if we correctly identify as the whole multiverse instead of the ego? That changes everything! God is the multiverse. God has complete free will. You are God remember. So at the highest level you as God do have free will. At the human level you do not have free will.

From the correct perspective of being the entire multiverse (God, consciousness) you can just let everything flow. Everything is happening perfectly, so you do not need to resist what is. One can surrender to what is. The more you identify as an ego the more suffering you will have in the game. When you identify as the multiverse you are very accepting of what is. This means not resisting life and just letting it play out. As God you do not need to change anything. **You knew exactly how life would play out before you incarnated into the game. You freely allowed yourself to be incarnated. This means you entered the game with your free will.**

In summary, the question of do you have free will or not depends on what perspective you look at it from. From the ego's perspective, no you can't control what is. From the perspective of the entire multiverse (God), yes you do have free will. God is controlling everything. He is using his will to create perfection itself.

Unconditional happiness

Is it possible to be happy no matter what happens? No, it's not. If you have experienced the loss of a loved one you know how terribly sad we can be at times in this game. Tragedies occur and they can push us into deep sadness. Source wants to know what that feels like, so that is part of the game. But can we massively increase the amount of happiness we have in our game? The answer is a resounding yes!

Often people say "I'll be happy when such and such happens." Or they say "I'll be happy when I don't have to do such and such anymore." This is how most of us operate. It is called outcome-based happiness. We will be happy only when an event occurs. The problem with this is that it may not occur. Or it might occur, and you are happy for a short while until you need something else to occur. It keeps going like this. Your happiness is dependent on external events.

An example of this is a story I once heard about a guy called Tom. Tom suffered from the condition known as "keeping up with the Joneses." He envied his next-door neighbour who had a very nice car, a late model BMW. Tom was quite open about the fact he wanted one too. He already had a good car, but in his mind, he felt he needed a BMW and then he was sure he would be much happier. Tom saved his money, mainly by cutting back on social events and entertainment. After 2 years, he had enough money to put a good amount of money down as a deposit on the car. He got a personal loan from the bank for the rest. So, he bought himself a brand new, black BMW. Tom was over the moon with this purchase, and he proudly told anyone who would listen just how happy he was to have this new car. He openly admitted that he had wanted to keep up with his next-door neighbour. Both Tom and his next-door neighbour used to park their cars halfway up their respective driveways. Two black BMW's side by side. They looked a treat together. Three months had passed since Tom had bought his new car and then something happened that shook Tom's world. Tom's next-door neighbour had got rid of his BMW and instead halfway up the drive was a red Ferrari. He had upgraded! Tom suddenly wasn't happy anymore. All that time he was chasing after money because he thought he would be happier with a new car. Only to find his happiness disappeared when his next-door neighbour trumped his black BMW with a red Ferrari. A classic case of outcome-based happiness turning sour.

An alternative to outcome-based happiness and a much better way, is to say, 'I will be as happy as I can regardless of the events that occur in my life." It is much better to appreciate all the good things we have in this game. Appreciate the small things in the game and the things many take for granted. Do you have a bed to lie in at night? When you open the refrigerator door is there food inside? If the answer is yes then, allow yourself to feel gratitude for these blessings. For some people the answer may be no. Then we have to look at even more fundamental blessings. Are you warm right now? Do you have a safe place to sleep tonight?

Do not focus on your problems. There are always going to be many people in the world worse off than you. You have probably heard the expression; "first world problems." Many people may be in a situation where they would love to have some of your problems.

Try to move away from outcome-based happiness. Feel as much gratitude as you can regardless of what's happening in your life. A positive attitude helps. I recently heard a great example of positive thinking in regard to our age. The quote was "Today is the youngest you will be, for the rest of your life." This flips on its head the old adage "Another day, another day closer to the grave." Sometimes, it just takes a change of perspective.

The very best thing you can do to be happy, is to transcend living through your ego (the individual self) and this book covers this in depth in Chapter 2 The Egoic Self and Chapter 4 Become Spiritually Enlightened. This is the ultimate goal.

I am now going to give some general advice to improve your happiness. It won't make you as happy as you would be if you transcended your ego, but it will certainly help until the moment comes when you achieve spiritual enlightenment. This is personal development stuff and it can start helping you straight away.

Chasing pleasure will not bring you happiness. So, forget about drinking, taking drugs, overeating, constant sex, buying things all the time or whatever your addiction might be. These things bring only temporary pleasure. These things will give you a spike of dopamine in the brain and you feel good. The problem with this though is the dopamine hit doesn't last and because of this you have to repeat the hit over and over and now you have an addiction.

Rather than chasing pleasure and increasing dopamine it is better to do things that increase serotonin in the brain as serotonin brings a kind of happiness that lasts much longer than a dopamine hit. The advice that follows will help you increase the serotonin in your brain.

It helps if you have some meaning in your life. You need to have some reason to get out of bed in the morning, some purpose. To have this purpose you need to align your career and lifestyle with your highest values. For example, you might have the following highest values of exploration and new experiences. If these two things are your highest values, then you need to set up your life so that you do things every day that are congruent with these two values. In this example the perfect job or career could be being a pilot, aeroplane host or travel guide writer. In this way the person has a reason to get out of bed because their career and general life is aligned with their highest values.

The opposite is also true. If your highest values are in conflict with your career or general life, then you will be unhappy and have no purpose. An example of this may be a vegan who values the environment and animal life. This woman works in an abattoir, slaughtering cows. Do you think she will be happy? Of course not. This is an extreme example, but it highlights the importance of aligning your career and general life with your highest values. When you align these two areas you have purpose in life, and you will be much happier.

It is a good thing to spend some time thinking about what your values are. Everyone is different so everyone will value different things. Spend some time thinking this through and write them down. You might want to come up with about 6 or 7 things you try to live your life by. **These are values, things that resonate with you at your core**. These are the values you attempt to make congruent with your career and general life. These values may change over time, so be flexible with them. My six highest values at this time of writing are; freedom, adventure, integrity, kindness, frugality, authenticity. For me freedom encompasses everything from financial freedom to personal creative expression. Adventure to me involves making every day a great experience. I have a love of travel so I try to travel as often as I can. One of my goals in life is to travel to 50 capital cities of countries around the world before I die. I have aligned the way I live so that it is congruent with my values.

Happiness requires cultivation. By that I mean you must design your life in such a way so that you are doing things every day that make you happy. Happiness is who you are and how you live. You must become aware of those activities in life that you enjoy and then do them. You need to be self-aware to do this. Here is a list of questions you will need to know the answer to in designing your life:

How much time in nature do you want?
How much sex do you want?
How much socialisation do you want?
How much variety in life do you want?
How much do you want a successful career?
How much time do you want with your partner and family?

Do you want to do something which involves leadership?
How much spirituality do you want?
How much learning do you want?
What hobbies or interests do you want?
Do you want to be your own boss?
How much time alone do you want?
How much creative expression do you want?
How much risk do you want?

Find out the answer to these questions and then **design a life which gives you exactly what you want.**

There are certain activities or habits that you can cultivate which are known to increase happiness. Below is a list of things which will help:

Good food, Exercise
Self-care (looking after yourself), Meditation
Laughter, Travel
Facing and overcoming your fears, Donating to a charity
Doing unpaid charity work, Having me time
Helping others, Having a healthy lifestyle
Having a nice custom-made living space
Having a pet, Study or research
Being selfless, Being authentic
Expressing love, Integrity
Loving yourself, Attitude of gratitude
Mastery of managing money, Developing your spirituality
Using your talents, Having a hobby.

There are also certain activities or habits which are known to decrease your happiness levels. Below is a list of these things:

Excessive pleasure seeking, Drugs and alcohol
Chasing fame or celebrity status, Lying and being dishonest
People pleasing, Chaos in your life
Living in an unpleasant environment, Narcissism
Criminal activity, Not working or overworking
Addictions, Abusive relationship
Dysfunctional family environment, Perfectionism

Not managing money well, Gossiping and drama
Intolerance and judging people, Not being authentic
Being a victim, Chasing material items
Procrastination, Eating junk food
Not facing fears, Too much partying

These pointers pretty much speak for themselves. I want to explain one of them however. That is **chasing fame or celebrity status**. A lot of people do this. They dream about becoming famous. It is a trap to fall for this. Famous people are not inherently happier than people who are not famous. Ask yourself the following question if you are someone chasing fame. Why do I want to be a celebrity or to be famous? The answer if you are honest with yourself is because of your ego. The ego wants to be special. It wants to be put on a pedestal and it believes fame will provide that.

You do not need external approval. Having your own approval and having high self-esteem is better than having the approval of thousands of fans. There is a brilliant song by The Stone Roses entitled "I Wanna Be Adored." This song title sums it up. The ego thinks that by being famous people will adore it and that will feel good and increase its feelings of self-worth. I am saying it probably won't and that you are better working on increasing your feelings of self-worth inherently by loving yourself and respecting yourself.

Another point I would like to make is something which affects a lot of people. You may have some chronic health problems or a disability. Perhaps you have a mental illness. One in six people have a mental illness and many people develop a physical health problem at some point in their lives too. To be happy you must accept that you have this condition and make peace with that. Do what you can to help manage the condition and try to make the most of each day. Whatever you do, don't fall into the trap of feeling like a victim because of a challenge like this. If you do this, you are just going to make it even worse because you resist what is. One must surrender to God or to the universe. This means accepting your condition and being at peace with it.

As I have already mentioned I have two chronic health problems myself. Sarcoidosis (an autoimmune disease) and Fibromyalgia. I also have mild anxiety. These conditions take a real toll on me. Especially the fibromyalgia which causes me pain throughout my body and complete exhaustion if I try to do too much. At the beginning I resisted the fibromyalgia and that caused me immense emotional suffering. I was a victim angry at the universe. Why me? I would say. Why have I got this horrible health? I was so ill that I could no longer work full time as a teacher. So, I lost that job and the income from it. Because of this my wife and I were forced to sell our dream home as we could not make the mortgage payments anymore. This made us both very sad. It was a testing time for our marriage.

I was ill for six years not knowing why before I was finally diagnosed with Fibromyalgia. I resisted all this time. It took another five years before I finally surrendered (out of utter despair) and accepted that I have to live with this disease. However as I mentioned earlier that suffering I experienced was actually my teacher as it caused me to look within, out of this utter despair. **When I looked within I suddenly found God** and then my life immediately changed for the better.

You may know of the late actor Christopher Reeve who played Superman in the Superman movies of the 1980's. He unfortunately broke his neck in a horse-riding accident and was instantly paralysed from the neck down. This wonderful man was able to make peace with the universe even after losing all movement from the neck down. This is so remarkable because he could easily have become bitter and depressed. It would have been so easy for him to be angry and wonder why a loving God would let this misfortune befall him. Instead, he accepted and surrendered. This is an inspiring example of how to deal with a severe health challenge. You can choose to be happy no matter what happens to you.

I will end this chapter just re-iterating that there is a lot you can do to increase your levels of happiness. You just need to be self-aware enough to know what things give you happiness and then design a life full of these things.

The ultimate happiness comes from transcending the ego and attaining spiritual enlightenment and I will explain how to do this in Chapter 2 The Egoic Self and Chapter 4 Become Spiritually Enlightened.

Let go of attachments

Attachments in simple terms are those things in the game we decide we must have. It could an object, an experience, a lifestyle, a skill or something completely different. We cling to these attachments. We want them at all costs. They become a big part of our identity.

The problem with attachments is that they often cause suffering. Often we struggle just trying to keep hold of these attachments and if we can't keep hold of these attachments we suffer terribly when they slip through our fingers.

A lot of people are attached to their job. They will suffer terribly if they lose that job. Some people are attached to their partner. Losing your job or losing your partner is a severe shock to the system but it is easier to cope if you are not attached to these examples. You must be able to say to yourself something like this "I love my job and my partner but if I lose them my life will carry on and I will still be okay."

Here is an example of an attachment: Kate is a woman who has always viewed herself as a musician. She has been a long-time member of a very successful punk band called Porridge. She is very heavily attached to this identity. She has in the past felt a lot of pride from being a musician in a popular band. This all sounds great and there is absolutely nothing wrong with being in a band. It only becomes a problem when you heavily invest your self-worth into being in a successful band. Let's say in this case the band break up permanently and Kate is now feeling lost. Let's say she cannot ever again find another band that are anywhere near as successful as Porridge. Kate is at a loss. She no longer has the identity that she once had. She feels empty.

Another example is Hong who decided in his 40's he wanted to get fit and so he joined a gym. This is a great thing to do. Hong improved his health quite quickly. Hong was so pleased with his results that he got seriously into body building. He trained every body part twice a week. He supplemented with various products and followed a very strict high protein, low fat diet. He managed to build a very impressive muscular physique. Hong enjoyed his new body and it really helped his confidence and self-esteem. It doesn't sound like a problem at all does it? The problem only came a couple of decades later when in his 60's his health deteriorated due in part to the steroids he had been secretly taking. He was too sick to train at anywhere near the intensity he had been doing for years. He was not able to take the steroids either. It wasn't long before the fit and muscular body was a thing of the past. This would not necessarily be that terrible but for Hong this was his greatest fear come true. He had become attached to being big, strong and muscular. He now hated his body. He longed to have his old body back. He had become completely attached to his old body and was utterly miserable now that had been taken away from him. Obviously, weight training is a very positive and healthy thing to do but again, if you become too attached to anything you suffer terribly when you can no longer do it.

One more example is George. George grew up in a well to do family. It was certainly upper middle class and possibly higher, close to the top 1% of average net worth. He went to private schools all the way through his childhood and never knew financial hardship. He went to university and graduated with a business degree. After this he joined the family business which was a chain of video rental stores. He filled the position of general manager initially and after several years moved into the CEO position replacing his mother who at this point wanted to step down and enjoy retirement.

He was on the whole an astute businessman and was very competent running the business. He had an ego which drew pride from being a businessman and having wealth. His ego drove him to want more and more money. So, he decided to expand his video empire and opened up new stores. Not just a few but twenty new stores up, down and across the whole country.

His ego wanted him to become even wealthier. He wanted to become a multi-millionaire, well and truly in the top 1% of the wealthiest people on the planet. He had to borrow money to do this, and he borrowed a lot of it from his bank. The expansion went ahead and George was working 15-hour days steering the ship. Initially it went well but unfortunately it wasn't long before his video empire hit choppy waters. The problem was all of a sudden people weren't buying DVD's anymore. The world was changing and people were streaming movies online. Websites like Netflix had started to become very popular and people were simply not going into video rental stores to rent DVD's anymore. George didn't know what to do. He had enormous debt and his business was failing. The banks wouldn't lend him anymore money.

What happened was that the business went broke. He had nothing to pay his staff in wages. He had to close down all his stores. He even lost his own house because he had re-mortgaged it in a desperate attempt to keep two of his better stores open. Suddenly George had nothing. He had no money at all. With no house he had to move back in with his parents at age 45 and he was devastated by what happened. All his friends were wealthy types and he felt shame and embarrassment around them. This shame and embarrassment came from his ego. His ego couldn't take his huge descent from wealth to poverty. It punished him with guilt. He avoided his rich friends and pulled back from his entire circle of friends because he felt like a failure.

There is nothing wrong with being wealthy and nothing wrong with expanding a business but when the ego latches on to this to pump you up, then you are going to take a tumble if you lose that wealth somehow. This is what happened to George. It was his ego that made him take the big risk of a massive expansion of his business. If it wasn't for his ego he would have been more careful and prudent running his chain of video stores. Just like the other examples, George had become too attached to something. In this case he was too attached to having money and wealth.

Can you see in this last example how two faced the ego is? It was the ego that pushed and pushed George to expand his business but when the business failed, the ego changes position and crucifies George with guilt for expanding the business. The ego wants it both ways. Imagine if George had a friend who talked him into expanding the business. What would George think of his friend if the friend turned around and blamed George if the expansion failed? Some friend! Yet this is how the ego operates. It tells us to do things and if it doesn't work out it then casts the blame on us and it (the ego) gets off completely free.

We are wise if we do not invest all our self-worth into one or two things because there is always a chance that we might lose them. Then how will we feel? Probably quite empty. It's good to have interests and the like but its best to be more rounded with a range of interests. If we do find we are focusing too heavily on one thing, then we should pull back and reassess.

What are you attached to? Be honest with yourself. What do you pride yourself on? It just takes a bit of introspection and honesty to realise what your attachments are. Consider that it is possible that you will lose this attachment and prepare for that by trying to loosen your attachment to it and find self-worth from other areas of your life.

Beginner's mind

Imagine if you saw a flower for the very first time in your life today. Imagine you had never seen one before. This was your very first up-close look at a flower. Would you not find it captivating and beautiful? Every flower is a miracle. Every flower is beautiful. It is just that we have seen so many in our lives we take for granted how beautiful each one is.

Beginner's mind is a concept which comes out of Buddhism, and it explains how we have names and classification for everything. So, we don't really see things properly. We see an object with a name, and even then, that name comes under a classification. Because of this, we miss out on the raw beauty of seeing something that we can't classify.

Let's keep the example of a flower. We all know what a flower is. This familiarity reduces the beauty and wonder that we should feel every time we see a flower. There are over 400,000 types of flowering plants in the world. Each with their own name. Then there are categories of flowers and sub-categories of these too.

Let's look at a wild rose. They are over 100 types worldwide and we humans have named and numbered them all. The classification of a wild rose is as follows....

Class:	*Magnoliopsida*
Superorder:	*Rosanae*
Order:	*Rosales*
Family:	*Rosaceae-Roses*
Genus:	*Wild Rose*

We do this with everything not just roses. Everything has a name and number. This kills the authenticity and the wonder of the world around us.

Buddhism tells us to see things with fresh eyes and calls this beginner's mind. Practice looking at the world around you with fresh eyes. Imagine seeing something for the very first time and feel the absolute wonder of playing this game.

Imagine you were born in a land-locked country and had never seen a beach before. Imagine you had never even seen a beach on TV or in any book. You literally had no idea what a beach was. Now imagine if you then took a trip to Hawaii and first stop was Sunset Beach just when the sun was going down. You are standing right there at the water's edge. Can you imagine how that would feel? It would take your breath away. That is what beginners mind is. That is the type of awe we can feel from really seeing something without classifying it first.

Remember you are everything you see. When you look out at the world, you are looking out at your divine self.

The higher-self

Each soul has what is called a higher-self, looking over it. The higher-self (also sometimes called the true-self or oversoul) has not incarnated into this game. It resides in the spiritual realm. The higher-self is infinite and eternal. A soul may experience a long life on Earth, but this is experienced as an instant flash to the higher-self. Every incarnation by a soul has first been agreed upon and then planned out in conjunction with the higher-self.

We will learn later in this book that there are possibly an infinite number of different versions of your soul living within a multiverse. Each soul having different life experiences. The higher-self can be thought of as the summation of all these souls. All of these souls having these experiences come from the higher-self.

If you are wondering how you relate to the higher-self, that is a great question, and the answer is quite astonishing. **The higher-self is a version of your soul from the far future.** A far more evolved version of the soul. This higher-self turns back in time to guide versions of itself earlier in its evolution. So, your higher-self is you. It's just the you that you will be in millions of years from now. Remember that time is an illusion. It does not really exist and that is how this is possible.

So, the higher-self is an extension of yourself which exists in the spiritual realm. It can come down from heaven into your soul here in the game if it chooses to. It will do this if it wants to experience something in life more fully.

I have had one experience when this happened to me. I was with my wife on holiday in Hanoi, Vietnam. My wife and I decided to do something which for us was very adventurous and a bit crazy. Anyone who has been to Vietnam knows that there are in practice no road rules and that driving there is very scary for anyone not used to the traffic chaos. We decided to hire a motorbike and with my wife on the back I rode at rush hour through the busiest part of the city including a huge roundabout. It was one of the most scary and fun things I've ever done in my life mainly because I have never ridden a motorbike in my life before. This was the first time. It was a high octane, high adrenaline, fifteen minutes. The Hanoi roads were jampacked with cars, trucks, motorbikes and bicycles all weaving around somehow not hitting each other. During the 15 minutes on the motorbike and another 15 minutes after, I felt my higher-self enter into my body. It is hard to describe what it felt like but the best I can say is I felt ten feet tall and bullet proof. I felt full of life, more alive than any other time in my life. It was a majestic experience. My higher-self simply wanted to fully experience this fun, crazy moment.

The higher-self is made of energy and light and it contains all the information and wisdom from every soul in the multiverse that it oversees (remember there are possibly infinite versions of yourself in parallel universes within the multiverse and your higher self oversees all these different versions of you). As you grow in wisdom so does the higher-self. The higher-self is the form you will re-join with after your body dies in this game. It is the true you. **This is the form you will be in heaven between incarnations. All the other versions of your soul from all the other parallel universes, all go back and re-join with your higher-self once their incarnations are over too.**

The higher-self has achieved the perfect balance of the divine feminine and the divine masculine. Even though the perfect balance has been achieved it will usually present as either feminine or masculine. If your higher-self is male say, then most of its incarnations will be to male beings but not all. It will still incarnate as a female too but just not so often. You may be able to take a guess at which gender your soul leans to. Some men for example are very in touch with their feminine side. These men probably have a female higher-self. Some women may have attributes which are aligned with masculinity. Perhaps their higher-selves are male.

Attributes which are usually thought of as being part of the divine feminine include; love, nurturing, compassion, emotional strength, cooperation, right brained, good at forming relationships. Attributes which are usually thought of as being part of the divine masculine include; strength, leadership, responsibility, action, left brained, independence, logic and reasoning. We all have a mix of both divine feminine and divine masculine qualities. Look for these qualities within yourself as this is a way you can guess which gender your higher-self is.

Part of our journey is working towards having a better balance of both the divine feminine and the divine masculine. Remember the higher-self has the perfect balance but you do not. By looking at the qualities I have listed above, you may be able to pinpoint some qualities where you may be lacking and work on those.

Personal development and enlightenment

I highly recommend becoming interested in personal development to improve as a person. Throughout this book I explain that to find happiness and overcome emotional suffering one needs to transcend the belief that you are an individual person and see yourself as a divine soul instead. But sometimes you need to walk before you can run.

I recommend embracing personal development at the same time as you embrace spiritual development. This is a two-step process:

Step 1 - Get involved in personal development. Read books, attend seminars, get a life coach. Do all these things so that you can be a better person. This is time and money that you are investing in yourself, and it will deliver you many rewards. It will make your life better, but it will not take away all your suffering that comes from identifying as an individual person. To do this you must move from personal development to spiritual development.

Step 2 - Get involved in spiritual development and ultimately achieve enlightenment by transcending the ego (the belief you are an individual person). Chapter 2 - The Egoic Self and Chapter 4 - Become Spiritually Enlightened will give you all the information you will need to transcend this belief.

These two approaches are not mutually exclusive. **They can 100% be used together.** There is a paradox here. Step 1 tells you to develop the person. Step 2 says the person doesn't exist and that you need to transcend it. They seem contradictory and they are, but from a pragmatic approach they both can and do work together. It can be explained by this statement below:

Develop the person until you reach the point where you are ready to transcend the belief you are a person.

Personal development can be seen as a first step on the way to enlightenment. It doesn't mean you need to spend years on Step 1 before you start Step 2. No, you can do both steps at the same time. They will work together just fine as long as you are fine with the seeming paradox.

Perhaps the most important thing you can learn from personal development is that you are **at cause** in your life. **You are responsible for the results you get in life so don't blame others and don't blame fate.** If your life seems like it is a total mess, then it is your fault not anyone else. This is a big step because a lot of people haven't made this step and they cast blame at everyone else for what's going on in their life. You are steering the ship and you have the power to create any kind of life you want.

You might say " Hey it's not my fault that my business failed! The banks wouldn't lend me the money I needed to get the business thriving! Also my competitor used dirty tactics to make my business look bad. It's not my fault that happened!" Well actually it is your fault. Blaming others is easy but if you are really honest we are 100% responsible for the results we get in our life. So sure, it didn't help that the bank didn't lend more money and it didn't help that a competitor played hard ball but you still could have succeeded despite these obstacles. That's the real truth.

We all have obstacles in our life and we must navigate around them. It is not just business, its family life as well. It's all areas of our life. We must move from being a victim to being "**at cause**." In the driver's seat 100% responsible for our results in life. This is a mature, grown up approach. It feels good to live like this. For many, this way of living will require a major change in the way they live their life but if you make this change you have stepped up in life. You have gone to a whole new level and here is the truth; very few people have made this step up.

You might say again "Well, what if I get a chronic disease or what if my wife dies! I certainly didn't make these things happen!" This person would be correct. Of course no one is at fault in these cases. These things are sometimes called an act of god. No one is at fault in cases like these. Another example might be an earth quake or a flood. In situations like these even though it's no one's fault you are still **at cause.** You now have to carry on living.

You may be in a period of mourning for a while and that's perfectly normal. This must play out fully. Usually time is required to allow the healing process to play out. This could be a substantial amount of time. However at some stage you have to let go of the past and carry on. The first thing you must do is **accept** whatever tragedy has occurred. Once you have become able to accept what has occurred you must now **make peace with it** and carry on living.

No one can do this for you. Counselling may help even medication can help but ultimately you again are the one who has to steer the ship. So you are back again **at cause**. The alternative is to never accept what has happened, become angry with the universe and feel bitter for the rest of your life. No one wants to live like that but the truth is that there are many people who do never come to terms with an act of God. These people suffer for the remainder of their life.

I myself have two chronic illnesses. I have Fibromyalgia and Sarcoidosis. These two illnesses have a real impact in my life. Especially the Fibromyalgia. It causes pain in my body and I very easily become totally exhausted. The exhaustion can last for days. However I have now accepted it and I have made peace with it. It still causes me physical pain but it doesn't cause me any emotional suffering anymore. I make the best of all the good things I do have in life which are very many things. I have adopted **an attitude of gratitude**. I do actually believe I would not have adopted this attitude had I not got ill. Fibromyalgia was my teacher. I really believe that.

I now realise that the Fibromyalgia helped me in my spiritual journey too. It caused me to suffer emotionally at the beginning. I suffered terribly for quite a few years. It took six years before I was even diagnosed and I was very angry with God all this time. Eventually though, this suffering became so bad that I had a spiritual breakthrough. I had an epiphany and I found God. I looked within myself to find some answers to the big questions about life. I had started seeking and I was laser focussed in my quest.

Suffering has this effect on people. If you have a perfect life with no pain then it's not very likely you will want to seek out the answers to the big questions in life. Why would you? You are just happily going on with your wonderful, perfect life. No need for help from God. No need to search for anything.

By the way, very few people have this kind of perfect life. Almost everyone suffers at different stages of their life. This is the way life is meant to be at this level of the game we are playing. The Buddha himself said that to live is to suffer. He was able to eventually transcend suffering and become enlightened. Believe it or not you can do this too. This book will tell you how.

I will come back to this topic later in the book but for now let's just say that emotional suffering causes people to look within and seek out the meaning of life. They also want to escape from the suffering. This is possible if they seek long enough. The way they are finally free of the pain is the day they attain **spiritual enlightenment**.

So this is why there is so much pain and suffering in the world. It's like this because it almost forces people to look within and be a better version of themselves. It forces people to cry out to God for help like I did. It forces people to seek and when they seek they almost always uncover and find out

way more than they bargained for. They will find out that it is possible to live with no suffering at all but the only way to do this is to become spiritually enlightened.

A lot of personal development gurus will tell you to lead what they call a big life. They encourage you to make huge amounts of money and to have a massive impact in the world. I don't prescribe to this philosophy. Firstly, I will say that there is nothing wrong with being rich and nothing wrong with having a big impact in the world, but I don't believe it is for everyone. Some people may simply want personal development to be a better person. Or to be a better husband or a better mother.

An important lesson I learnt from personal development is that if you get angry or annoyed by the actions of someone else, it is because you have the same capacity within yourself. The other person is mirroring a flaw you have within yourself. So, instead of just getting angry, ask yourself - why am I getting angry? What is it in myself I am seeing in this other person? Then the next step is to come to terms with that flaw within yourself and heal it. If you do that you will no longer be triggered into anger when you see someone else demonstrating that same flaw in character.

Here is an example. I know someone who is very tight with money. This person takes frugality to the extreme. I believe frugality is a good thing but when you take it too far it's not such a great thing. This person is probably the tightest person I've ever met. They never pay for anything unless they absolutely have to. It used to really bother me. A lot. However I learned through personal development that it bothered me because the extreme frugality was reflecting back a flaw inside myself. This could mean that I am tight myself or it could mean that I have some concerns/worries, guilt or unresolved beliefs about money and generosity. In this case it was the latter.

I had unresolved beliefs about money and generosity. At this time in my life I was contributing to five charities with monthly payments. I believed that everyone should be doing this too. This is the belief I had that was misguided and this is what caused me the frustration I felt towards this person. To resolve the problem I had to gently question and soften this expectation. I realised that people are shaped by fear, upbringing and survival. Not everyone thinks the way I do. I even realised that I was giving away too much money and that I could not afford all these charity payments.

This didn't mean I was approving of stinginess; it just meant I released the need I had for others to meet my own inner standard at the time. The next step was to turn the mirror inwards and work out why I had such a high standard in the first place. **It was because I had a limiting belief that being generous would make people like me. I also had a limiting belief that giving money to charities is a big part of being a spiritual person.** I used the limiting belief blaster in the appendix of this book to remove these two unconscious limiting beliefs. Now I have healed that flaw within myself. I am no longer bothered by people who are cheap. I can choose to be generous myself because it feels aligned by love, not because everyone should be.

This is not easy. I will say it again just to really reinforce this idea in personal development. If you get angry or annoyed by the actions of someone else, it is because **you have the same capacity within yourself**. The other person is **mirroring a flaw** you have within yourself. It's a radical change. Whenever you get upset by someone's behaviour you have to put the spotlight on yourself. You have to put yourself under the microscope. This is hard. It's hard to do especially in the moment when you are angry with someone but you can do it.

One of the most important things you can learn is to love yourself. I read the absolutely brilliant book by the late Louise Hay entitled; "You can heal your life." In it she writes about an activity you should do every day called mirror work. Mirror work is standing in front of a mirror looking at your face while you repeat out loud "I love myself, I love myself." While you repeat this mantra, what you must do is feel that emotion of love for yourself. I can't stress enough how powerful this is and how much it really does help you learn to love yourself. When I first tried this myself, I couldn't bring myself to do it such was my own self-dislike at the time. So, what I did initially was say "I like myself, I like myself." I did this for a period of time until I could bring myself to say "I love myself." This is a very powerful process. I strongly encourage you to try doing this and make a habit of it. The key is to really **feel the emotion** of self-love as you do it.

I have found that to love yourself, you must be prepared to forgive yourself for mistakes you may have made in the past. Everyone makes mistakes. It is impossible not to so it's important to learn to go easy on yourself. Cut yourself some slack because just like everyone else you are doing the best you can. A good way to forgive yourself from mistakes you made in the past is to do mirror work and instead of saying "I love myself," say "I forgive myself."

To forgive yourself you need to let go of emotional baggage that you have been carrying around with you your whole life. Let go of that baggage. Just drop it and live in the moment. In Chapter 2 - The Egoic Self, there is a section on mindfulness which will help you live in the moment. The past has been and gone. There is no need to carry that emotional baggage around with you. Just decide to let it go.

Many people are like a backpacker who walks around with a huge backpack on their back except their backpack is full of emotional stuff from the past. They are bent over by the weight of it. They can hardly function in the game because of the weight of the backpack. Imagine that you are this backpacker and you have just arrived at a train station to travel to the next destination. Imagine just dumping the backpack and leaving it on the platform. Take it off, leave it on the platform and jump on the train without that heavy weight on your shoulders. That is what you must do. Free yourself from your emotional baggage from the past.

Carrying the load of that backpack is hard because the backpack most people carry is very heavy. It serves no purpose to ruminate over the past. This is just a game we are playing here, so treat it as such. As I have said no-one is perfect. We are literally built to make mistakes. That is how we learn. Later in this book you will learn that this game we are playing is a holographic computer simulation. It is not even real and you as a separate person is also not real so all the more reason to not care two hoots about mistakes you have made in the past.

In Louise Hay's book "You can heal your Life" she also writes about the power of affirmations. Affirmations are short positive sentences for us to recite either in our mind or out loud. Here are a few examples of useful affirmations to recite...

I deserve all the good that life has to offer **(Abundance)**
I deeply and completely love and accept myself exactly as I am **(Self-Love)**
I forgive myself and others, and I set myself free **(Forgiveness)**
I am willing to release old patterns and choose peace instead **(Peace)**
I trust the process of life & everything I need comes at the right time **(Trust)**

There is a trick with repeating affirmations. You don't just say them over ten times then stop. The trick is to recite them and at the same time attach or feel the emotion that matches the affirmation. For example:

I forgive myself and others, and I set myself free

When you recite the affirmation above, really feel the feeling of **forgiveness.**
Turn up the feeling of forgiveness really high. This massively increases the
power of affirmations. I have put in brackets above the emotion or feeling
you should feel deeply for each affirmation listed. Reciting affirmations will
make it easier for you to drop that backpack of negative emotions and
negative stories from the past.

I have found that it does help to have long-term goals in life. Goals can
give you motivation and purpose. I believe that if one does not have purpose
then it's much more likely that one will be depressed or harbour a lot of
negative emotions. I have a goal of visiting 50 capital cities around the world
before I die. I also have a goal of helping 1000 people with this book within 3
years of publishing it. If the book sells better than I hope, I will change my
goal so that I am aiming to help more people than 1000. If it is not selling like
I hope, I will reduce the number of 1000 people to a lower number.

Decide what long-term goals you want in your life and write them down.
This gives you purpose and something to work towards. A good goal needs
to meet certain criteria. There is a useful acronym to help you write your
goals. It is the **S.M.A.R.T.** acronym. These letters work as follows: <u>S</u> (Specific)
<u>M</u> (Measurable) <u>A</u> (Attainable) <u>R</u> (Relevant) <u>T</u> (Time based).

You can see that my two goals are written in such a way as to encompass
the 5 criteria above. You need to write your goals in the same way and make
your goals congruent with one or more of your personal values (this is what
the <u>R</u>- relevant aspect means).

Remember that values are those attributes that you live your life by. As I
mentioned earlier it's a great idea to have a think about your values and
write them down. It gives you something to live up to.

Here is another goal I have set for myself and my wife; *I wish to buy an
apartment in either Bali or Vietnam once my wife turns 60 and then both of
us will live there and retire from all work.* Once again it encompasses the
S.M.A.R.T acronym. **Specific**- Bali or Vietnam, **Measurable**- I will be living
overseas, **Attainable**- We can afford to do this by using our Australian
superannuation savings, **Relevant**- this is congruent with my values in
particular freedom & adventure, **Time based**- when my wife turns 60 and
can access her funds.

Personal development is about growing as a person. Often, we harbour
fears that hold us back from that personal growth. In fact, many of us have
fears like this. To grow as a person, sometimes we need to face our fears and
overcome them. This is not easy. These fears can be so bad that the thought

of facing them causes the palms to sweat and the heart to beat hard. But the longer we avoid our fears and procrastinate over facing them the worse they get. Some of these fears may have been holding you back over many life times. The fear would have been getting stronger and stronger with each incarnation.

There is only one way to overcome a fear. That is to do the thing that you are fearful of and to do it more than just once. You need to do it 3 or 4 times in a short period of time. You may be aware of the book written by Susan Jeffers entitled; "Feel the Fear and Do It Anyway." It is an excellent book.

It is scary to think about facing fears and that is why one thing is required to help us face our fears. That one thing is **courage.** When we use courage, we are scared and that is why we need the courage. The benefit of overcoming a fear is enormous. It is like a weight has been lifted from your shoulders. It is like you can breathe properly again. Yes, you can avoid whatever the fear is, but it will hold you back. It is always in the back of your mind chipping away at you. This is called living inside your comfort zone. There is no personal growth to be had within your comfort zone. I love this quote:

"Life begins at the end of your comfort zone" **Neale Donald Walsch**

This quote speaks for itself. All the growth and all the magic of truly being alive comes from stepping outside of your comfort zone. Courage is the key thing. Bottle up some courage, feel the fear and do it anyway.

The biggest fear I have had which I have managed to over-come is the fear of public speaking. When I was a kid I never had this fear but it developed in my late teens. The thought of standing up in front of an audience and speaking terrified me. All those eyes watching me while my voice quivered and my hands shook. I didn't want this, so I avoided it at all costs. This fear I had for a long time, over ten years. There were times at university when I had to speak because I couldn't avoid it. I would just stumble through somehow saying the very minimum possible. I would be a nervous wreck doing this. I was avoiding it at all costs.

After university, I began work as a high school teacher in New Zealand. Teaching obviously requires a lot of public speaking so it was in a way forcing me to confront this fear. But I continued to avoid it all costs. For some reason I wasn't afraid of speaking to the kids at school and I was fine in class. It was just the adults (the other teachers) who terrified me.

For three years I hardly ever spoke up at the daily teacher meetings which took place every morning before school started. I never spoke at the regular full staff meetings. Then one day I was forced to because the principal asked me directly to present to the whole staff. I was absolutely terrified. There was no way out. I stood up and faced the staff of about 40 other teachers who were all sitting silently looking at me. I started speaking about the subject matter and within seconds I felt absolute terror. I should have spoken for a good few minutes but I think I stood up for about 20-30 seconds.

After stammering out a few sentences I went into a full panic attack in front of my colleagues. I was unable to speak anymore. My heart was racing. I was shaking. My voice wasn't working, and I dived back into my chair. Back then I had never heard of a panic attack before. It was years after I realised there was a medical term for what had happened to me. All I knew was that I had humiliated myself in front of my work mates. It was a very embarrassing moment in time. I think the principal felt sorry for me because he never asked me to present to the staff again.

Even after this I still hid from this fear. It was probably another year before I realised I really had to beat this fear. I made the decision to face this fear and beat it. I forced myself to speak to an audience 4 times in a period of about 48 hours. At the morning meeting I put my hand up and spoke out loud while sitting in my chair giving some short information about the rugby team I coached. I was smart enough to keep this to a short announcement so I could build some confidence from it. It worked. Then when I got home, I rang up a talk back radio station and spoke about something in the news at the time. Even talking on talk back radio terrified me but I kept talking for about 4 minutes even though I was shaking and my voice was quivering.

The next morning at school I spoke again at the morning meeting. This time I spoke for a longer period of time. I was gaining confidence. That same day we had a full staff meeting after school. I took it upon myself to stand up and read out a prayer to commence the meeting (this was the way this Catholic school started all meetings). All of this did the trick. The fear just melted away. I can speak from my own experience that beating a fear is a wonderful feeling. It is a feeling of liberation.

I am sharing this story because this is the textbook way of beating a fear. Start off slowly facing your fear a little bit and then gradually expose yourself a little bit more, then do it again and again in a short period of time. Four times in 48 hours worked for me (I am now a very good public speaker) and it will for you too.

"What we think to be our greatest weakness can sometimes be our biggest strength." **Sarah J Maas**

Personal development when you boil it all down is about growth. Growing as a person. It is best when you grow in all areas of your life not just one or two areas. There are six aspects to personal development. This means there are six areas of your life where you can experience growth. The six aspects are:

Physical
Intellectual
Financial
Relational
Emotional
Spiritual

There are entire books you can read extrapolating on how to grow in each of these areas. For the purpose of this book, I am just going to give one example of an activity you could do in order to grow in each aspect. Of course, these are simply examples of one possible activity. You will choose something that you are interested in or that you wish to explore.

Physical - Start a regular walking regime.
Intellectual - Learn a new language.
Financial - Learn how to do a detailed budget.
Relational - Make a new friend.
Emotional - Don't take criticism personally.
Spiritual - Practise meditation.

You don't have to do this all at once, but it is good to try and grow in all six areas. Growth is important. If you stand still and don't grow, then you stagnate. It is a constant process as you never stop growing. A lot of people focus too much on one area. It can often be financial. If you are focused just on making money you will be out of balance because all these areas are absolutely vital and you should not neglect any of them.

To grow and develop the self you will do well if you live out those six or seven values I spoke of earlier in the book. It's all very well to write down six values and it's another thing entirely to actually live them out.

One of the most difficult of all the values to actually live up to is **integrity** (the quality of being honest and having strong moral principles). I have singled this value out because it's so lacking in this world. I would love you the reader to master this value. Do you know someone in your life who has integrity? If you do I would predict that you have a lot of respect for that person.

If you want to have integrity then if you say something you must always follow through. You must be honest, ethical and consistent in your actions, doing what you believe is right even when no one is watching. Integrity requires a lot of effort. It is something that many human beings do not have. I include myself as a person who has not had much integrity for a long part of my life. Many times in my life I have not followed through with promises. I have demonstrated poor behaviour and been less than honest.

Interestingly our pets have more integrity than we do. Take a cat. It will scratch you or even bite you if it feels like it has a reason to. It will purr and sit on your lap if it feels like it too. One thing it won't do is deceive you or lie to you. It's honest and consistent in its actions. It doesn't play games like us humans do. It operates with full integrity. Of course our lives are more complicated than a cat and that is why integrity is hard to keep up. It requires cultivation and real commitment.

To improve the self you must be self-aware. You need to get to know yourself. You need to understand if there are some behaviours that you exhibit that are not what you would like them to be. Be brutally honest with yourself. What areas of your life need work? Are you a people pleaser? Are you fake (living behind a mask)? Are you judgemental? You can't remedy the problem unless you are self-aware enough to know you have that problem in the first place.

Do you know that a lot of people do not know themselves even after a whole lifetime? Most people cannot recognise patterns of thoughts and behaviours that they exhibit in life. You are most probably more thoughtful than most people or else you wouldn't have bought this book. You definitely can get to know yourself. You can do this with introspection/critical analysis and again brutal honesty. Do this at the same time as you come to terms with the truth that there is no self.

I once attended a personal development seminar in Melbourne, Australia. It was an awesome seminar. In it we played group games. These games were fun but it was all about growing as a person. We learnt lessons through play. Then people would go up on stage and tell everyone what lessons they had learnt or what experiences they had had. One thing the main speaker of the seminar insisted upon was that he wanted no one to use the word "**try**". He actually quoted Yoda from my favourite movie series, Star Wars. In it, Yoda said;

"Do. Or do not. There is no try." **Yoda**

If anyone used the word "try" while on stage they had to perform ten press ups straight away. You can guess why he had it set up like this. When we try to do something we are telling the game that we might fail to do it. When we don't try but say "I will do something." We are telling the universe that it is going to be done. There is no doubt.

Let's say you are going for a big job interview. Don't say; "I will try to get the job." Say instead; "I will get the job." The universe listens carefully to what we think and the words we use. If you use certainty as I have above you are more likely to get the job. To start with you are in a better frame of mind; "I will get the Job." You go into the interview confident and expecting success. The universe picks up on this and guess what? It gives you what you said you will get. In this case you get the job.

It's actually hard to not use the word "try." Most people use it all the time. But here is the thing. If you can erase it from your vocabulary you are setting yourself up for more success in life.

There is yet another word that can cause problems or actually upset people. It's only a tiny word. It is "**but**". You may think that it's a pretty harmless word and most of the time it is but in certain conversations it has the power to upset the person you are talking too. Here's an example;

"Hey Joe, I like the work you did yesterday. It was well written **but** it did sound a little tired."

Let's break down what Joe will mostly feel about this feedback. It is highly likely he will only focus on the part of the feedback that comes after the word "**but**". Humans operating through an ego-based operational system will only think about the negative part of the conversation. Joe will only think that his boss feels his work seemed tired. This is just the way the human ego works. It focuses on the negative and will hardly register the positive that preceded it.

In this case Joe will gloss over the fact that his boss liked his work. He will also gloss over the fact that his boss thought his work was well written. That's two pieces of very positive praise from his boss. Despite this he will not feel any pride. He will only be thinking about what comes after the word "but". **When you use the word "but" in this type of way it has the effect of negating everything that came before the word "but" and it highlights the words that come after the word "but".**

In this case Joe will probably have taken offence that his boss thought his work was tired. **He's totally forgotten about the good things his boss had to say because the word "but" has negated them.**

Here are a couple of other examples where the word "but" can possibly upset a person;

*"Hi Carol, you look good today. I like your dress **but** the colour is a bit unusual"*

*"Hey Dave, great performance from your band at last night's gig. You guys rocked **but** for some reason the vibe felt a bit off"*

You can see how the ego will most likely react in both examples. It will get defensive. Carol and Dave may feel slighted and they simply would not have heard the positivity before the word "but".

Can you see how this word is not helpful? A lot of personal development gurus will tell you to use it as little as possible. It's exactly the same for the word "however". It has the same effect. The thing is though, quite often we do need to use these words. It is actually quite hard to not use them. You will notice that right here in this book I have used the word "but" many times. This will not upset you though because I am not speaking or writing about you in particular. I am speaking in general terms and not especially about you.

Sometimes it can work to replace the word "but" with the word "and". This could work with the example above of Carol. Contrast these two statements;

*"Hi Carol you look good today, I like your dress **but** the colour is a bit unusual."*

*"Hi Carol you look good today, I like your dress **and** the colour is a bit unusual."*

Can you see how much softer and more positive the second version is using the word "and"? The use of this word changes everything. It implies that the unusual colour is possibly a good thing. It also does not negate the words before the word "and". Whereas the first version does and the use of "but" implies that the unusual colour is a bad thing.

What I am going to say next is a big one for me. It is about saying sorry. It's about making an apology. When you apologise, ditch the "but". "I am sorry but…." isn't a real apology. It's a half excuse. Just say "I'm sorry" and mean it. That is how apologies actually work. Consider this example below and think about which one is a true apology:

"I am sorry Abdul"

"I am sorry Abdul but you were really pushing my buttons"

The second apology is not even a real apology. It shifts attention away from your remorse and onto the other person's behaviour. The apology becomes conditional, almost a justification, and the emotional impact of saying sorry is lost. A true apology is simple and clear. It is unambiguous; "I am sorry". It acknowledges responsibility without qualification or defensiveness. When we drop the "but" we give the other person the full gift of our accountability and our sincerity.

The ego loves the "but"(we will learn about the ego in the next chapter) because it wants to protect itself, explain itself, or defend itself. In doing so, it sabotages connection, trust and genuine remorse. Learning to apologise without "but" is a small but profound way to practice honesty, humility and authentic personal development.

You may be thinking that you need to erase this word from your vocabulary. No you don't. Sometimes you do need to say "but" or "however" and that's okay as long as you are saying it with **conviction.** That is the key. **Only use these words in the manner we have been discussing when you are speaking with true or strong conviction.** The definition of conviction is "a firmly held belief or opinion, especially one that you feel strongly is true and are confident about, even if others disagree".

I would like to end this section on personal development with three inspirational quotes about personal growth:

"One can choose to go back toward safety or forward toward growth. Growth must be chosen again and again; fear must be overcome again and again." **Abraham Maslow**

"Twenty years from now you will be more disappointed by the things you didn't do than by the ones you did do. So throw off the bowlines. Sail away from the safe harbour. Catch the trade winds in your sails. Explore, dream, discover." **Mark Twain**

"I learned that courage was not the absence of fear, but the triumph over it. The brave man is not he who does not feel afraid, but he who conquers that fear." **Nelson Mandela**

Chapter 2
The Egoic Self

This is not psychology

As we discuss ego in this chapter, we are not doing it from a psychological place. In psychology ego is classified as ego, super ego and id. There are seven different ego states too. We are not using ego in that way. We are just using one word which is ego.

We are not using it in the way some people use it when they say someone has a "big ego." That's not it either. This is just one possible expression of the way we will be using it.

What is ego

Ego is like a software program running in your head. It identifies with the body, the mind and memories. It says, this is me! It's the bundle of thoughts you have about the individual person you think you are. Everything about you that makes you, you.

So, ego is the picture you have of yourself. Your body, your mind, your personality, your strengths, your weaknesses, your memories, everything that makes up this seeming human being. It's true that you have all these things, but the ego says that you are these things. You could say it's your operating system that you use to interact with the world around you.

But here is the thing. This ego is not real. It is just an illusion. You are really a divine soul as explained earlier and because you have undergone the veil of forgetting, source needed to give you a fake self, for you to believe in for a while.

This fake self has a voice which is constantly commenting in your mind. This voice is running you and pretending to be you. It is your overall sense of self. It is to whom you refer to, when you start a sentence with the word "I" or you use the word "me."

So, let's be really crystal clear about what I'm saying here. Right now you think you are an individual human being (an ego). I am saying that you are not. The individual person you think you are, is a fake self. You were given this fake identity because of the veil of forgetting. There are no separate or individual people living a separate life. There is only life itself and you are life itself pretending to be a person. So now this book will help you stop believing you are an individual human being and start remembering that you are a divine soul who is one with everything in the game. You are everything in the game. You are everything on Earth and every star and planet in the multiverse. Everything means everything. You are all of it and its all one and it's all God. Remember the cosmic joke that makes an enlightened person laugh? They are laughing because they are far more than an ego. They are every single thing that exists in the entire multiverse.

It is likely that you, even after reading that still believe you are an individual person or ego. This book is going to help you let this belief fall away. Sometimes people who are chasing enlightenment believe they must kill the ego. The first thing to realise is that we cannot kill the ego. This is a misperception in spiritual circles that the ego must die. No, you cannot kill the ego. It is not possible. You just have to learn to live with it. If you get egoic thoughts just ignore them and let them pass. Don't grab hold of them and ruminate over them. Let them be.

We have an ego because of the veil of forgetting. Life on Earth would be very different if we knew we are God. So, to avoid this, the ego was created so we could identify with an individual self until we were ready to learn the truth. There is an apt acronym you can make with the letters in the word ego. That is:

E-*edging*
G-*God*
O-*out*

It is true that if you are identifying as an ego, you can't correctly identify as God at the same time, so yes you are edging God out.

The ego lives in the mind. The average person has up to 6000 thoughts per day according to a recent study by a team of psychology experts at Queen's University in Canada. Out of these 6000 thoughts any that refer to the person is ego.

The ego tells you that you are incomplete. It likes to make comparisons and find you lacking. It will make you feel weak and like a victim. It tells you that happiness is just around the corner, but it never is. Let's explore why ego makes you suffer.

Why identifying with the ego makes you suffer?

The main reason why you suffer is because the ego is often very negative. Some people will be more negative than others, but ego is just inherently negative. It usually only ever describes our life's circumstances based on fear, doubt and lack. We find all these negative takes on playing the game of life very tiresome. The game becomes heavy and hard dealing with these negative mind programs. Nothing seems to be good enough. The ego is over critical. It compares you to others and finds you lacking and this is exhausting in itself.

Emotional suffering is the result of the ego's constant internal commentary running in your head. Challenging things can happen in life but often this self-talk from the ego makes these challenges even worse. You might feel physical pain from some accident for example. This is bad enough, but on top of this your ego has decided someone else is guilty of causing this to happen. So now, as well as the physical pain, you have emotional pain too. In this case, anger at the person who did this, as well as a sense of being a victim. Often, in examples like these, the emotional suffering is the worst part.

Most of the time, for most people, there is a quiet suffering happening. Most people have been suffering at a low level throughout their whole life. They have been doing this for so long, they don't realise they are suffering. It has become just normal life for them. It's a pervasive feeling of dissatisfaction in life. A faint feeling of not having really lived up to their potential. A kind of constant disappointment with themselves. This is just what comes from living as an ego.

A funny thing about the ego is that often it doesn't matter how much we achieve; the ego still wants better. There are some people who achieve really great things but inside their ego is saying they could have achieved even more. There are other people who lead what could be called a mediocre life. Perhaps they have been in the same safe job for 20 years. Their ego is quietly and subtly just chipping away at the person telling them that they could have been so much more. The ego in these cases is telling the person they have failed, they are not good enough, they have wasted their lives. People live with this. They are so used to their ego putting them down they are not consciously that aware of it. They wonder why they are irritable and why they get angry. In a nutshell their ego is telling them they are a failure.

The ego as mentioned earlier lives in the mind and our minds are set up in a way which is very negative. We have a lot of negative thoughts and these thoughts come with negative emotions as well. I can list many negative emotions which come with the ego. You will well know emotions like regret, disappointment, shame, embarrassment, humiliation. It is ego which is behind these negative emotions. The ego is built in such a way as to bombard us with emotions like these which kind of piggy bank on to negative thoughts. Sure, we can have positive thoughts too but if you are honest, you will recognise that we linger on or dwell on negative thoughts much more than positive ones. This is emotional suffering.

It doesn't matter what you achieve the ego wants more. You might get a promotion at work for example. Say you got a team leader position. You will feel great for a while but soon your ego will be saying you could be general manager. It goes on and on like this. The ego never gets to the point where it says "all good, your life is perfect you don't need to do anything else just relax and enjoy. You have climbed the mountain there is nothing more to achieve."

What is it in your life that your ego is telling you that you "should" do? If you are honest, you will recognise the ego is quietly telling you that **you are not enough at this moment in time.** It will likely compare you with someone else and find you lacking compared to them. The ego loves to compare. It might say that your best friend has a better job than you or that your brother-in-law has a better house or a faster car than you. It could be that when your brother-in-law bought that car you felt a pang of jealousy along with a thought that he now has a better car than yourself. These kind of thoughts happen to everyone. People won't admit things like jealousy openly, but it bubbles away beneath the surface. This is how the emotional suffering goes. The ego views life as a competition. It wants you to win but no matter how well you go, it will still want more. A better job, a faster car, a grander house. Even when you get these things, the ego will be sure to find someone else who has got a better version of these things.

In my own personal life, I experienced a lot of this when I worked for three years as a real estate agent. The firm I worked for deliberately used money earned from the job to rank every agent in the firm. There was a large whiteboard in the General Manager's office which displayed highest to lowest the names and total earnings for the year from each agent. Everyone could see exactly how much money in commission each real estate agent had earned for the current year. The owners of the firm were deliberately relying on ego to motivate each agent. They were deliberately creating competition between the agents. It was a straight-out competition to see who could earn the most money. Do you think that those real estate agents down the bottom of the list didn't suffer emotionally? Of course, they did. I was one of them. I was not one of the higher performing agents and I knew exactly who was above me and who was below me on that whiteboard. My ego wanted me to go up as high as possible on that list. If one of my colleagues had a big sale, I would congratulate them outwardly and appear to be pleased for them but deep down inside my ego was killing me and telling me that I must now sell more houses to keep up. At this time in my life, I was completely under the control of my ego and this job was quite simply awful. It was a terrible setup, and I was pleased to be out of it once I stepped away from selling real estate.

It is not always material assets that the ego focuses on. It could be something like creative ability. Perhaps a friend of yours was recognised for an art piece she created. Your ego might say "why didn't I create an art piece as good or better than her." The ego will focus on whatever it is you deem important, be it creative ability, looks, career, intelligence, whatever. The ego will compare and contrast you with others and it will find you lacking. That is the guarantee. It will find you lacking no matter how well you do.

I am deliberately using the word "suffering" as this word is used in Buddhism, to describe exactly what I'm talking about here. In Buddhism we are taught that everyone suffers at different times during their life and the only way to transcend this suffering is to become spiritually enlightened. In Chapter 4 - Become Spiritually Enlightened, I will explain what steps you can do to realise this for yourself.

This all sounds depressing, but there is good news. We don't have to identify with this individual person the ego tells us we are. We can transcend ego and play our game as a divine soul (or if you prefer God). To do this we identify with the God part of us and give up all the drama that comes with taking oneself so seriously as a person. You can give up all the drama of not being enough, of not having enough. You can give up all the drama of being in a competition with everyone else. It's a much better way to play. Instead of silently suffering, we can begin to shine. Of course, we still use the words "I" and "me." It's just we don't identify as being the separate individual person. We use these words for convenience and to navigate this game. As you read on, I will explain how you can do this.

How ego is a catalyst to bring us freedom

As mentioned above living in ego brings suffering. People can suffer for a very long time. Certainly, a whole lifetime. In fact, people can suffer for hundreds or even thousands of lifetimes. But at some point, they reach the end of their tither and say "enough!" They can't take it anymore. At this point they are experiencing an existential crisis or a spiritual crisis. This is often the beginning of a spiritual awakening. From here the person will start seeking. When I say seeking, I mean the person will seek out information about who they are, what is the meaning of life and why are they here. They want the answers to the big questions. This seeking usually goes on for a period of many years. This seeking will eventually set them free from suffering but to be truly free the seeker must go all the way to spiritual enlightenment just like the Buddha did. This book will tell you what you need to do to go all the way. Spiritual enlightenment is a real thing. It is the prize that all spiritual seekers want. It is the end of suffering and the beginning of happiness. Real and sustained happiness.

This is how ego eventually self-destructs. After many lifetimes of pain, a burning desire starts to come through. A burning desire to find meaning in life. A desire to know who you really are. People get to the point where they will do anything to stop the suffering even giving up their own personal identity. Because that is exactly what is required. They must give up their very own identity. What this means is that the person stops identifying as the person and instead identifies as God. This is who you really are. **Your true identity is God and when you realise this for yourself, you break free from suffering and you attain spiritual enlightenment and lifelong happiness.** If you are reading this and don't believe you could give up your personal identity, you may surprise yourself.

First of all, what you need is desire. Work on cultivating that desire to be free. It is also a desire to know the truth. **It is the emotional suffering that comes from believing in an ego that forces us to seek the meaning of life.** Because of the suffering we begin to desire knowing our divine self and this is how consciousness evolves. The truth is you are a divine soul. So, all you are really doing is aligning yourself with the truth. It's always been the truth. You have always been a divine soul, it's just you hadn't realised it. You were still hanging on to the ego.

You cannot just instantly give up the ego and believe you are God. For the majority of people, it takes time, and it even takes practice. Some few people instantly drop the ego and never go back, but this is rare. The great spiritual teacher Eckhart Tolle is one such person. For most of us it happens over time. Often two steps forward then one back. But don't be discouraged as it is do-able. As you read this book you will gain valuable information that will help you transcend the ego given time.

Ego just wants you to identify with it

All the ego wants is for you to believe you are the individual person. It is terrified that you will realise you are God. It doesn't care if you are feeling pain or something pleasant, as long as you are thinking about being a separate individual. This is the way it sustains itself. This is how it continues to exist. It uses the emotions of **pride and guilt** as its two main weapons to keep us focused on being the individual person.

Ego will often find things in the game which it uses to make us identify with it. The positive things that are claimed by the ego are often those things we are good at. For example, one person may be very physically attractive and they derive part of their sense of self from being attractive. This will be a source of pride for the ego. The ego will keep this person dialled in on their looks. If they are thinking about their looks, it means they are associating with the individual person.

Ego can identify with negative things too. It will find aspects of ourselves where it feels we are lacking and then it will exploit that to just make us focus on being the individual person. The ego will guilt trip us on these aspects of ourselves. An example may be a person who has come to believe he is lazy. He may beat himself up with guilt when he is sitting on the couch watching TV. All the time he is sitting on the couch beating himself up he is identifying with the individual person, and this is all the ego wants.

As I mentioned above the ego's main two tools are pride and guilt. It uses both tools to make you identify with the individual self. Consider this example below of Arjun who is good at sports. Because he is good at sport, Arjun's ego will be hypersensitive to anything involving him playing sport.

Let's say Arjun is a good golfer and he gets beaten in a round of golf by someone who is just learning the game. Expect a strong negative emotional reaction. Being beaten didn't go down well as his ego finds him guilty of playing badly. The guilt that the ego piles on will also lead to other negative emotions coming through like shame, embarrassment, and frustration to name a few.

Let's say Arjun is playing against a semi-pro golfer and this time he wins. In this case the ego will make Arjun feel pride. This time Arjun will feel really good about himself for a period of time.

The important point here is that the ego doesn't care whether Arjun wins or loses at golf. All it wants to do is continue to survive as the ego and it simply wants Arjun to continue to identify with it. In both cases above Arjun is feeling a strong identification with the individual self. This is all the ego wants.

Each person has something that their ego attaches itself to. It could be sport, intelligence, looks, body, job, artistic or creative abilities or basically anything. These are your potential triggers. You will be highly sensitive around these attributes which are important to your ego's sense of self.

There is also such a thing as a collective ego. This is where a group of many people all identify with something. The most obvious examples are countries. Every country in the world is made up of people and those people living in the country have a collective ego. They usually identify as a citizen and often they are patriotic towards their country. Patriotism can be a good thing but there is a danger that this identification with a country can become too strong and that can be a bad thing. Taken to an extreme this patriotism can become more like nationalism which is dangerous. Nationalism is often the cause of disputes and even wars between countries. What I am saying here is that when you boil it all down ego is the cause of wars. It is not just countries where the collective ego comes in to play. It is cities, regions, even sports teams. Many people identify so much with a sports team that they suffer and have a miserable week if their team happens to lose at the weekend.

If ego is causing us suffering, why does it exist?

The ego is a result of natural selection and evolution. It came about at roughly the same time our ancient ancestors created language. It is a modulation of our fight and flight system. It was created once humans became more self-aware and social.

The main reason it came about was to keep us alive and to make us reproduce. It does a good job at that. Early humans hunting or gathering for food would know to run if they encountered a lion. So, the ego gives us that survival instinct. Because the ego is inherently negative this helps us stay alive. That is why we run from lions. If it was more positive, we would be less likely to run from dangerous situations. Being negative is the safest way to stay alive.

The ego allowed us to have some form of self-awareness although not true self-awareness. It allowed early humans to have names to distinguish one from another. It also allowed for the concepts of past, present, and future to exist. Having an ego is a necessary step in evolution. Those people that have cats or dogs for pets will know that these animals respond to their name because they are developing a sense of self or an ego. We need to develop a sense of self or ego so that we can operate as a human being in this life. We need to know our name and recognise our face in a mirror. This identity has helped us play this game. This is a first step only because this is not who we really are. As I have already mentioned it is a fake self, developed because of the veil of forgetting we undertook before incarnating in the game.

Being an ego is useful for a while. It is a step along our evolutionary journey. It has helped us humans play this game for a long time, but we are now reaching a point in our evolution where it is no longer necessary. We need to move beyond this. We are no longer hunter gatherers. Our lives have become far more complex. The time has come for us to upgrade from an ego-based operating system to a God-based operating system. We will still respond to our name of course. It's just that in the back of our mind we will know that this is not who we really are. **We are really every single thing in the game. Every single thing is one and every single thing is God.**

Ego wants us to climb up the social hierarchy

As well as survival, ego has another function. It wants us to climb up the human social hierarchy. As early humans became more self-aware and social, the brain needed to evolve to keep up with this. The ego became more complex and intelligent and status in the social hierarchy became very important.

This desire to do well socially is linked to the survival function of ego because those people at the top of the social hierarchy get all the good stuff. They get the best food, the best shelter even the best mate. This means they are also more likely to survive.

So, the ego has done a great job at keeping us alive over time. The problem is we don't really need it like we used to. The chance of being eaten by a lion is close to zero for most of us living in cities. Likewise, the desire of the ego to climb up the social ladder is causing more harm than good. Many people have stress and mental health issues because of this drive of the ego for us to be more social.

A very common mental health concern is social anxiety. Hundreds of millions of people suffer from this. It is the drive from ego that creates so much invisible but powerful pressure to succeed socially. Forget being eaten by a lion, for many attending a child's birthday party can be a more anxious event than a lion on the loose. This type of fear can seem even worse than the prospect of being a lion's lunch.

Let's continue with this kid's birthday party example. Say a socially anxious man attended a kid's birthday party and he said something that he instantly regretted. Some eyebrows were raised from other parents. This man's social status has been challenged. The ego wants this to happen. Why? Because the man is suddenly very self-conscious. He is right now strongly identifying with his ego or individual self. He will be feeling guilt straight away.

Why does the ego use guilt so much? For survival reasons once more. The man has made a mistake so now his ego punishes him with guilt so that he remembers this incident and doesn't make the same mistake next time. The ego does not want the man to slip down the social hierarchy so from its point of view, it is helping him survive. Guilt is the ego's weapon. It only ever wants to focus on self-preservation and keeping you high up in the social hierarchy. So, if anything happens which may affect your social standing the ego piles on the guilt.

Sometimes the ego decides someone else has treated you badly and it will find this other person guilty. This is why you feel anger or frustration or another negative emotion towards certain people. They have been judged guilty of bad behaviour. It has become you versus them. So, you are identifying again with your ego. This time you are feeling slighted by this other person. The ego doesn't care what you are feeling just as long as you are feeling something and are identifying with the individual self.

I want to explain again why the ego uses guilt on you when you make a mistake. Two reasons: firstly, so that you identify as the individual person or ego and secondly so that you learn from your mistake and don't make the same mistake again. This second reason of helping you learn from your mistake is linked to the ego's desire to keep you up the social hierarchy. I will say it again. From the ego's point of view, it believes it is helping you. But the greater truth is that the guilt is making you miserable and it's making you suffer.

The ego lives in the mind. It is all the thoughts in the mind that refer to you as an individual person. Let us now examine more closely this mind we all have. Let us critically examine these thoughts that we all have about ourselves.

The Bogeyman

Do you automatically believe your thoughts? I have mentioned earlier in the book that we have 6000 thoughts per day. Most of us believe each thought to be true. The problem with this is that in fact our thoughts are usually not true at all. Often our thoughts are wide of the mark. So why are we automatically believing in them? This causes us a lot of emotional suffering especially when we believe negative thoughts about ourselves. These negative thoughts are really only perceptions. The definition of perception is the way in which something is understood or interpreted. So, when we think, we are using perceptions to assess a situation or other people or ourselves, these perceptions are not necessarily accurate, yet we automatically believe them to be spot on.

We are often far too hard on ourselves. Many of our thoughts are very self-critical. When we believe these thoughts, we suffer. If we could just stop automatically treating each thought as truth, we would save ourselves a lot of needless suffering. I ask you to be suspicious of your negative self-talk in the mind. Are these perceptions really accurate or are they too harsh on yourself?

I would like to present an example of a thought you might have had as a child. Were you told about the bogeyman? The bogeyman is a make-believe creature who comes after children if they are not good. This is something some children are told by their parents and is used as a way to scare kids into behaving themselves. If small children are told this by their parents, they believe it. They automatically believe it but is it really true? Of course, it's not true but as far as the kids are concerned it may as well be true because the thought of it causes them to suffer.

No adult still believes in the bogeyman, we now know it doesn't exist, but we believe other thoughts which are just as fictional as the bogeyman. A lot of children believe everything they are told but we as adults need to grow beyond this. I ask you to be highly sceptical of your thoughts. It is very likely that your perceptions are not accurate, and you are causing suffering for yourself by automatically believing thoughts that are false.

We need to get to the stage where we are always quite dismissive of the nonsense that comes from the mind. We need to be able to say to ourselves "oh that negative thought is just my mind at it again. I will take absolutely no notice of this nonsense." In this way we totally de-power the mind. Instead of believing every thought we treat every thought with suspicion. We hold just a kind of curiosity about what the mind has to say but we put no weight on it at all. This is where we want to get to. It does take time. We need to practice reflecting on what the mind has to say and then considering if it's really true. We need to be self-aware to do this. Meditation will help us gain that self-awareness and with practice we will be able to do this quite easily.

If you choose to believe a negative thought about yourself then you are making that thought a reality whether it's true or not. Take a beautiful woman. She might look like a model. She is tall, slim and beautiful. But this woman could have a thought or multiple thoughts that she has plain looks. This is not true, but she makes it true. By believing anything you effectively make it true. This woman will go her whole life truly believing she has plain looks not realising that many people look at her and see a beautiful woman. This is really common for men and woman. No matter how beautiful or handsome many people cannot see it in themselves.

It is not just looks, it can be anything. There are people who are really talented but their own thoughts hold them back. Maybe you can sing or you can act but you never try to pursue these talents because the mind tells you that you are not good enough. Perhaps you are intelligent but never decide to use your intelligence and study at university. I know someone who had a talent and passion for understanding weather, but he never pursued it because his mind told him he is better suited as an administration clerk.

What is it that you believe about yourself that other people would never believe? I can guarantee there are lots of things. Your mind is judging yourself far too harshly. It is telling you lies. Wake up and stop believing the rubbish which comes from the mind. Question everything.

Mindfulness

Constant thinking is making us miserable. There is a non-stop voice in our head that tries to make us associate with the individual self or ego. It is the habit of the mind to link thoughts together which creates the ego. We think it is a steady train of thoughts but really thoughts just arrive. This linkage of thoughts makes us believe we are a persona. These thoughts limit us and we suffer because of it. If only there was an off switch for the mind, then we could turn off these almost constant thoughts.

Of course, we need to think and we need thoughts. Thinking is needed as a tool in the game. About 10% of our thinking is useful, while the other 90% is mainly ego-based thinking and is not that useful at all. What I am referring to here is the 90% of ego-based chatter in the mind.

One of the best books I have ever read is "A New Earth," by Eckhart Tolle. In this book Eckhart says we are addicted to thinking. I found out from reading this book that thinking was causing me to associate with the ego. So, initially I thought what I needed to do was stop thinking. Literally, stop thinking. I tried to turn off all my thoughts, but of course it didn't work. No matter how hard you try, you cannot stop thinking.

After I finished reading "A New Earth," I realised I had to just let my thoughts be. Let the mind think and not give my thoughts any attention at all. Thoughts are like clouds in the sky. We are like the blue sky. Clouds come and go, and the sky lets them come and go. So, this is how to do it. Let the thoughts come and go. Let them be.

We are the presence that is behind the thoughts (the blue sky). We are the stillness that is listening in to the thoughts. We are not the thoughts themselves. Most people in the world believe they are the voice in their head. They are identifying with this voice. If you think you are the voice in your head, you are identifying as the ego and you have a big problem. A major switch in identity is needed. A switch from ego to divine consciousness. **You need to stop believing you are the voice in your head and instead believe you are the silent stillness which is simply listening in to all these thoughts.**

What do I mean when I say you need to switch from identifying with the voice in the head to identifying as divine consciousness? Divine consciousness is a word that describes the consciousness you possess as a living being. It is your aliveness. In spirituality it is often called awareness. Awareness, consciousness, aliveness all mean the same thing. We all have an aliveness. It's there in the gap between your thoughts. It's with you 100% of the time. When we believe we are the voice in the head we are missing out on enjoying being divine consciousness because we are totally distracted by thoughts.

Thoughts take you away from divine consciousness. A stream of thoughts if you indulge in them will take you back in time into the past regretting something or off into the future worrying about something. The point is that thoughts take you away from the present moment. **If you ignore thoughts and just be still in the present moment you are experiencing living in divine consciousness.** You are experiencing aliveness. This is a massive step forward if you can do this. Identifying as divine consciousness is what every mystic and every monk wants to be able to do. The problem that makes it difficult is that we get distracted by thoughts. We end up following a chain of thoughts and miss out on experiencing divine consciousness. This is why I want to help you put some distance between you and your thoughts. Thoughts can be alluring. They suck you in but mostly these thoughts are making you miserable.

You still need to think at times of course. It's just that you use thinking as a tool. Remember I said that 10% of your thoughts are useful and 90% is basically ego-based chatter. Practise using your mind as a tool for the 10% of things that are useful. Your mind is an extremely sophisticated tool. It is incredible when used in the right way.

One of the most powerful ways of taking your attention away from ego chatter in the mind and into divine consciousness is by putting your attention inside of your body. Become aware of the inside of your body. When you do this the ego chatter in your mind quietens right down. Let's try an experiment. Just now for the next 20-30 seconds, just put your attention on the inside of your body. Perhaps you can put your attention on your heart. Just remain grounded and unmoved in who you know you really are.

Did you notice that your mind quietened down and you had less thoughts? Were you able to feel the silent stillness of divine consciousness in between thoughts? **This silence is who you really are.** That silence is God. It doesn't matter if it was just for a split second. Even a very brief moment of silence is a start. With practice you will be able to do this better and better. So, the switch in identity I'm talking about is switching from believing you are the voice in your head to believing you are the stillness in your head.

The best way to summarise it is as follows:

You are divine consciousness (a divine soul) which is simply listening in to the voice in your head. You are not the voice itself.

It is good to practice mindfulness or as Eckhart say's "presence." Mindfulness or presence, is being present in the moment and not lost in thought. Become aware of the inside of your body. Do your best to be in the moment and not thinking about the past or worrying over the future. Use your five senses to be fully in the present moment. Look at what is around you. Pay attention to what is happening. Mindfulness is a habit you can cultivate. Practice it, so it becomes second nature for you.

You can operate fine in the world without relying 100% on thinking. Have you noticed that sometimes when you think, you are just telling yourself what you already know? Sometimes we have an instant knowing or understanding of a situation and we don't need to think it through. Often by thinking we just tell ourselves what we already understand. This means that we can understand without the need for thinking. The thinking is sometimes superfluous. We have an intelligence which is separate and independent of thought. When we are present, we still have access to this intelligence.

Presence is how we get in contact with that part of us which is always there. The unchanging awareness of just pure being. Presence is how we access our divine self. This divine self has been covered up by thoughts, perceptions, feelings, and images but presence brings us back in touch with this unchanging part of us that had just been covered up for a while. Presence is analogous to us undressing at night before we go to bed. Instead of taking off clothes, we take off thoughts, perceptions, feelings, and images revealing what was there all along. We do not become this pure being. We always were this pure being.

So being in the moment not lost in thought is the key. Allowing those thoughts to come and go without attaching our attention to them. Presence is another word for God. When we are present, we are one with our divine self. This is who we really are not the individual person that the ego tries to make us identify with. We will realistically get lost in thought at times and when we do this, we just need to redirect our attention back to the stillness that is presence. It takes practice and time to master this. So be patient with yourself. The benefits of being present and not caught up in the drama of the mind is peace of mind. A reduction in emotional suffering and the emergence of peace and happiness.

I can't reiterate enough the importance of practicing presence. I often remind myself to be mindful or present just randomly. The key is not to be worried about thoughts that come when you are practicing. That is very normal. Driving a car is a great chance to practice presence. When driving just be aware of everything around you. Watch all the activity on the roads carefully. There is something about driving a car that lends itself perfectly for practising presence!

I want to finish this section reiterating the powerful truth mentioned above.

Presence is how we access divine consciousness. It is the key that unlocks our divinity. In other words, presence is the tonic which helps us transcend the belief we are an individual person and reveals to us the truth that all along we were a divine soul just pretending to be a person for a while. In fact, it can be thought of as your superpower. The other great superpower you have is forgiveness. Forgiveness, like presence can free you from emotional suffering. The most important person to forgive is of course yourself. Forgive yourself at the same time you stop believing you are an individual self.

I am

Presence or mindfulness takes you into what is commonly called in spirituality the "I am" state. When you use presence, you enter the "I am" state and you are one with divine consciousness. "I am" is a term with an open ending. You may be wondering "I am" what? In fact, it is just "I am." The reason it's an open ended "I am" is because you are one with absolutely everything in the game. That is why it's open ended. So, you could say "I am everything."

There is another paradox however. We also know that this life is an illusion and that everything in the game is an illusion (we cover this deeply in Chapter 3 - We are Living in a Computer Simulation). So, if everything is an illusion then there is nothing really here. Based on this truth we could say "I am nothing."

That is the paradox. The best way to think of "I am" is to combine both ideas. So, we can now say that when you use presence you enter into divine consciousness and the "I am" state and the following is true...

I am everything and I am nothing.

Nothingness is an important tenet of Buddhism. Buddhists believe that all objects in the world are empty. This means there is no substance to anything. Again, this is the idea of matter being an illusion. Sometimes when you go into the "I am" state you can feel the nothingness of the game. It can produce feelings of bliss and peace. Who knew that nothingness could feel so good. Here is something that may surprise you – God's nature is nothingness. Yes, God at her essence is nothingness. The most highly evolved deity is nothing. It is hard to understand but it is so. God is everything in the game and everything in the game is nothing. There is nothing here. Nothing is really happening. This is advanced spirituality and it's not something we can understand with our finite minds.

There is another reason why the "I am" is an open-ended term and it's because the ego loves to classify itself with feelings or states. How often has your mind said things like; "I am no good at this" or "I am tired" or "I am so over this." The ego loves classifying itself with words. So, by cutting out these extra words we sidestep the ego. The ego doesn't know what to do with the "I am." Which is exactly why it's so powerful.

The "I am" state is something you can achieve. Presence or mindfulness is the key that unlocks the door to "I am." It is certainly a pleasant feeling when you are experiencing "I am." You are present in the moment. You are alert. You may have feelings of bliss or oneness and your mind chatter is not bothering you. As you grow and develop spiritually you will get better at experiencing "I am" and you will be able to hold yourself in the state for longer.

For now, I recommend practicing going into "I am." Take stock of yourself randomly throughout your day. Look around, observe closely. Feel the aliveness within your body. Feel your five senses. This is presence or mindfulness, and it is the entry point to "I am."

Here is a routine you could follow that may help you experience "I am." Try waking up ten minutes earlier each morning so that you can find time each morning to practice this routine. The routine is every morning before you really start your day but after you have showered and groomed, sit silently with your first cup of coffee or tea for the day. Sit and be as still as you can with your hot drink. This is really powerful. You will be very present in the moment. You will be doing absolutely nothing except for drinking your hot drink. Be as still as you can. Go into divine consciousness. Be aware. Be present. Be alive. Focus on the hot cup in your hands and enjoy the experience of drinking it. Really enjoy it and become aware of the experience of drinking a cup of coffee or tea. Make sure there are no distractions like television or your phone. Ideally you will be alone and doing absolutely nothing except drinking your hot drink. Thoughts will come of course but don't follow your thoughts, just let them come and bring your focus back to your hot drink. This is a fantastic way to start your day! You may have a busy household in which case you may need to find a room in your house where you can be alone. Make this a habit that you do every day.

Another way to enter into "I am" is to become aware of being aware. In spirituality the word awareness is often used instead of consciousness but they both mean the same thing. What does it mean to be aware of being aware? I will explain. You are aware all the time. At any point in time, you are using your awareness. You might be looking at something or doing something or whatever it is you happen to be doing. You are using your awareness all the time whether you are thinking about it or not. What you can do is become aware of your awareness. You allow yourself to kind of drop into this place. You can do this with practice. It is simply an introspection. Becoming aware of being aware.

When you do this, you drop into "I am" in a very deep way. You are in a place where you observe your own thoughts and emotions. You will find that you actually become present and you are not so troubled with a busy mind. This is simply one more very powerful entry point into "I am." It is even more powerful than simply being present. It is a most pleasant state to be in because you are simply observing all your thoughts and emotions instead of living inside them or being consumed by them. There is a level of detachment that comes from being the observer, thus you feel relaxed and calm. You will probably find that when you do this your whole personality changes. You are not riding on the crest of your emotions because instead you are in an observing position.

If you can drop into this place, you will notice that your thoughts quiet down straight away. Some people can go out into the world fully interacting with the world while they are aware of being aware. They can hold this state and live in it. I encourage you to experiment doing this. You may find that if you can do this a calmness comes over you. You will find you are not so bothered by negative emotions. In fact, you will be able to observe your emotions. In this state you are aware of any emotion that comes up. Being able to practice this is a huge achievement because when you do this you are not living in ego. You are very aware. You are very conscious. You are living in divine consciousness. Even if you can do it for short periods each day that is great. This is a great way to know yourself because it is true introspection. Like many things it is a habit you can cultivate. Some spiritual teachers call this "becoming the observer." This term is quite good because as I have mentioned you are indeed observing your thoughts and observing your emotions.

The great spiritual master Mooji speaks of becoming the observer. I recommend watching his YouTube videos on awareness. Mooji explains that it is possible to go even deeper than being aware of being aware. We are now getting into very advanced spirituality. Believe it or not we can go to an even deeper place. A place of utter nothingness. Here it is- you can become aware of being aware of being aware. This is not a word game or a joke, it's real. You might be confused by this so I will break down what this means. First you become aware of being aware. Hold this state for about 20 seconds and enjoy it. You have become the observer, observing your thoughts and emotions. Now ask yourself "can I go even deeper? Is there a greater presence which is aware even of this place?" There is such a place, and some people can just drop into this place, this is very advanced spirituality, and most people will find it difficult to access this state.

You are probably wondering how far back can you go with this. Actually it is what is called infinite regression. You can go back forever. The human mind can't cope with this though. It hits a wall. Conceptually the mind wants a last layer but there isn't one. The true nature of awareness is that it is self-reflexive and boundless. The layers are just pointers, there is no final layer because awareness already contains all layers within itself. **In true reality awareness never begins, never ends and requires no creation.**

Remember that awareness is another name for God. So the same applies to God. You may think; who created God? The answer is that God has **always existed**. God exists outside of time. Asking who created God is like asking what is north of the North Pole. It is conceptually meaningless, because God is outside temporal sequences. God was never created, it has always been.

So to recap, the mind likes layers but they are really just pointers to what the mind can't understand. It is still useful however to perceive these layers of awareness using the mind. The mind needs a handle or some stepping stones to experience awareness. Think of it like training wheels on a children's bike. These layers can help you to **rest directly in awareness**, without needing further conceptualisation.

I recommend practising this. Start with practising presence. Use presence in your life. This is the main thing. From time to time become aware of being aware and go deep into "I am." If you wish to become as still as possible then go deeper still and find the place which is aware even of this place. You just kind of drop into it. This ultimate place is utter nothingness, utter stillness. It is beautifully peaceful. It is the true nature of God. The best time to do this is alone in meditation when you can be very still and enjoy the feeling of nothingness.

This is a place that monks who have meditated for years may not even be able to find so don't be disappointed if you can't do this. You are not alone as most people will not know what I am talking about here. If you can access this place then that is great but if you can't don't worry, keep meditating and practice from time to time. Eventually you might be able to find this place and enjoy the utter nothingness. It is a most beautiful feeling. As I have mentioned this nothingness is the true nature of God so you are connecting with your true nature in a very powerful way. In face you could say you are becoming one with the ultimate creator, source.

Chapter 3
You are Living in a Computer Simulation

Pong

The year was 1979 and I was an 8-year-old boy when I played my first video game. The game I played was called "Pong" and it was the very first commercially successful video game ever invented. I played it on my childhood friend, Steve's television set. I loved computer games right from the off.

Pong was a simple game. It simulated a game of tennis. It was for two players. Each player controlled a rectangle shaped bat to knock a ball from one side of the TV set to the other. You could only move the bat up and down. The skill was to create the best angle off the bat you possibly could so that the other player would miss.

I thought that this game was the coolest thing I had come across in my 8 years of life. I was always keen to go to Steve's house to play. Steve was the only person I knew who had this latest piece of technology. All the kids in the street wanted to play it.

Pong was released on 29 November 1972. At the time of writing this book, it has been 50 years since this video game was released. This game was a hard act to follow, and it ruled the roost for several years but there were even better games to come.

The bar was raised significantly when the Japanese electronic game manufacturer Taito Corp released the brilliant game, Space Invaders in 1978. This game was a worldwide hit. It involved one player who could move a simple ship left and right and shoot down aliens, before they came low enough to crash into the player's ship.

It wasn't that long after 1978 that video parlours began sprouting up in the city I lived in, Christchurch, New Zealand. There was an arcade place near my house that had a games room featuring Space Invaders. I would bike there on weekends and after school to play this seminal game. It used to cost New Zealand 20 cents per game. I was sinking all my pocket money into this game. It was even better than Pong!

Space Invaders was also available on the Atari gaming console which was the only gaming system around at the time. To the current day, the Space Invaders franchise has netted over $100 billion dollars. To say this was an iconic game is an understatement.

These were heady days in the burgeoning video game industry. As technology improved better and better games were coming out every year. Some other classic games were launched. Games such as Pac Man, Donkey Kong, Defender.

Modern computer games

In the 50 years since Pong was invented, the power and complexity of computer games have exponentially sky rocketed. The current games of today are so far superior to Pong it's ridiculous. Current computer games are photo realistic, video quality, multi-player games. The multi-player feature means I could play here in New Zealand with other players from China, Germany, and Nigeria or anywhere else in the world.

In recent times we have been able to play virtual reality games. You can purchase virtual reality head sets and play games that mimic real life. This means players can experience being in a three-dimensional world and interact with that world while wearing the headset.

No one in their wildest dream could have predicted how vast the improvement of technology would be. The speed and power of computers have been doubling every 1.5 years since the 1970's. The key thing is that this increase in technology and the exponential improvements of games will never stop. All this has happened in only 50 years. In the grand scheme of time and humans on the planet Earth, 50 years is nothing. Not even a blip.

Computer games of the future

Based on what has already happened, it would be fair to say that computer games in another 50 years into the future will be beyond what we can even imagine. They will be absolutely astounding. The best games of today will seem like Pong to the kids in the future.

If the games from 50 years in the future will be unrecognisable, what will the games from 500 years in the future be like? Remember technology increases so rapidly. We just don't know what they may be like. Why stop at 500 years. What about 5,000 years or 50,000 years? The mind boggles at this point.

We can take a few guesses. There are already companies working on computer chips that can be put into people's brains. Elon Musk founded Neurolink in 2016, with the goal of developing a device that, after being implanted in a human brain, would allow a computer to translate a person's thoughts into actions. This is happening now, and it's only been 50 years since Pong was released.

So, given the vast improvement of computer games over time, is it highly likely that at some point, human beings will be able to create a computer game that can simulate life itself? For many people the answer is a resounding "yes!" If this is so, another question must be seriously considered. If the answer to that first question is "yes", how do we know that we are not already living in a computer game? How do we know that what we call life is not a game taking place in a very powerful computer from the future or from a higher power?

Simulation theory

The idea of our life being part of a computer game has been steadily gaining believers over the last few years. This belief is often referred to with the term "simulation theory." The founder of Neurolink, Elon Musk is a believer. He has said publicly, "If you assume any rate of improvement at all, games will eventually be indistinguishable from reality." Before concluding, "we are most likely in a simulation." Highly regarded astrophysicist Neil deGrasse Tyson agrees. He has said that there are "better than 50-50 odds" that the simulation hypothesis is correct.

Swedish philosopher Nick Bostrom has a fascinating view on this. He has talked about a stage of life he calls post human. The post human stage is when we are advanced enough to run human consciousness on silicon inside a computer. He has created a compelling argument which gives us pause for thought. He has said that **one of the following arguments must be true:**

1. The human species is very likely to go extinct before reaching a "post-human" stage (this could be some form of civilisation ending catastrophe like nuclear war or an asteroid striking the Earth).
2. Any post human civilisation is extremely unlikely to run a significant number of simulations (this could be for moral reasons or another reason).
3. We are almost certainly living in a computer simulation.

One of the three above assertions must be true. It is my belief that the most likely outcome is number 3: We are almost certainly living in a computer simulation. Nick believes that the creator of this game is likely to be the human species ourselves. Perhaps human beings from the future running what is known as ancestor simulations. This is just one possibility. It could also be an alien race. Could it be that the creator of our multiverse, is a highly advanced teenage alien, who created this game from his garage as part of a high school project? It is interesting to think about, but it is unlikely.

It is my personal belief that this computer game we are all playing right now was created by source. The big bang was literally source booting up the game. The first simulation was God's work but is this the actual simulation we find ourselves in? Let's think this through. The people in that very first simulation would have evolved just like we have. They would have invented computers just like we have and its extremely likely that at some stage they were able to run full simulations of life themselves. They were already in a simulation and then they develop their own simulation. Amazing, but does it end there? No, because eventually the people in that second simulation would develop their own simulation. So, we have a situation of simulations within simulations within simulations. It keeps on going like this. You have a kind of Russian doll situation of simulations existing within simulations. It is incredible to think about. Somewhere within all these simulations we find ourselves. Who knows where we are in the Russian doll. Who knows how many simulations there are above us.

If all this is true, let's think about a soul in the spiritual world planning out her life and about to incarnate into the game. She has the option of all these simulations to incarnate into. A smorgasbord of universes each subtly different from the others. She will choose which game is the best for her based on what her goals are. This is the stuff of a science fiction movie or book. What we are learning is that science fiction seems to be science fact.

Simulation theory may seem strange. It may seem to stretch your ability to believe in it, but it is congruent with science, philosophy, and spirituality. They can all exist perfectly together. I would like to now show how simulation theory answers many of the big questions we have.

The Goldilocks game

For life in this game to exist as we see it today requires a **statistical miracle.** Everything must be just right. For starters the Earth must be just the right distance from the sun so that it is not too hot or too cold. We must have just the one moon of just the right size as well. Thanks to its large size compared to Earth, our moon influences the length of our day through tidal interactions. The moon also stabilises Earth's axis of rotation, which in turn keeps our mild climate stable which is necessary for life.

The atmosphere of the Earth also happens to be just perfect. Not only does it contain the oxygen we need to live, but it also protects us from harmful ultraviolet radiation via the ozone layer. It creates the pressure without which liquid water could not exist on our planet's surface. It warms our planet and keeps temperatures habitable through the natural greenhouse effect. The atmosphere also protects us from small meteoroids that burn up upon entry.

Even the existence of Jupiter in the solar system helps us by protecting the Earth from asteroid and comet attacks through its gravitational pull.

The Earth also has a magnetic field which protects us from charged particles from the sun (solar wind). It also protects us from lower-energy cosmic rays which originate from supernova explosions, active galactic nuclei and other extreme astrophysical events. These rays are plentiful in our universe.

The strength of both the force of gravity and dark energy also happens to be just perfect. If gravity starting from the big bang was weaker or dark energy was stronger then stars and galaxies may not have formed at all. Conversely if gravity was stronger or dark energy was weaker then the universe would be very different and we would not exist. It seems like the values of every force and substance in the universe is perfectly tuned, exactly perfect to create life.

The strength of the strong nuclear force is also exactly what is necessary for life. If it was just slightly off we would not be here. The Proton-Neutron mass difference is spot on so that hydrogen and stars can be stable. Carbon resonance energy is also just perfect. If it was just slightly different carbon would not form in sufficient quantities and life as we know it would not exist. The initial entropy (disorder) of the universe at the big bang was extremally low without which stars and galaxies would not have formed at all.

Water, oceans and continents are arranged to recycle nutrients, regulate climate and sustain diverse ecosystems. Plate tectonics and volcanism maintain a stable environment. Even the Sun is perfectly stable, long-lived and made of just the right mix of elements.

The odds of all these factors combining and all of them being so perfect down to the tiniest of measurements is incredibly unlikely. Why has this statistical miracle occurred? Simulation theory provides a very neat answer. All the values of all the forces and in fact every aspect of the universe have been fine-tuned and programmed into the simulation we are currently playing in. The creator has designed every aspect of this universe so that life could flourish. All the settings were set in stone from the moment of the games beginning, at the moment of the big bang.

Computer code found in the equations of string theory

String theory is a mathematical theory which was created to have one single theory to explain our universe. It's often referred to as "a theory of everything." At present, we do not have one single theory to explain the universe. We have two theories instead. The first one came from Albert Einstein and it explains the large objects in the universe like planets, stars and galaxies and it does this very well. It is called general relatively. But it fails to explain what goes on at the level of the very small in the quantum world of atoms and subatomic particles. That's where quantum mechanics comes in. It is our second theory and we use quantum mechanics to understand what is going on at the level of the very small.

This all works very well but it is also very frustrating to physicists. It is because there should be one theory of everything to explain all the universe. We should not have to rely on using two totally different theories. So, this is why string theory has become so popular. It is an attempt to unite our two theories into one. String theory posits that at the very small level everything is made up of very tiny vibrating strings. String theory has made some progress but interestingly the equations of string theory only make sense when you allow for 11 dimensions to exist ("M theory;" the overarching string theory). We currently know our three dimensions of height, width and depth. The fourth dimension we all know is time. So, this means there are seven other hidden dimensions that are in play, but we cannot connect to them in any way apart from using mathematics.

There is something else that string theory is showing us. String theory predicts that there is more than one universe. It supports the view that there is a vast number of universes existing in a multiverse. I will dive deeper into multiverse theory and its ramifications later in this chapter.

One person has found something just as astonishing while diving deep into string theory. The theoretical physicist James Gates has claimed that he has identified what appears to be actual computer code (strings of ones and zeros) embedded deep in the equations of string theory. He has said they are very similar to what is known as error correcting codes. We use error correcting codes to make web browsers work.

So, when we look deep into the mathematics of the nature of the universe, we find computer code. If you believe in simulation theory, then this is not surprising at all. In fact, it is more evidence to support simulation theory.

There is another interesting area where computer code has popped up. Scientists in the field of genetics have discovered that our genetic code has a mathematical model just like as if someone (like a creator) had programmed it with a computer code. In fact, in 2017 a group of scientists at the university of Washington proved that they could embed computer code into actual strands of DNA.

What we think is solid is empty space

We think we live in a solid physical world. However, quantum physics has proved this to be wrong. When we look very closely at the building blocks of matter in this world (atoms), we find something remarkable. Atoms are 99.9999999999996% empty space. Everything is made of atoms, so this means **everything we see around us is almost entirely empty space.**

Every human on the planet Earth is made up of atoms. Each human has 7 octillion atoms in their body. This is a 7 with 27 zeros after it. Let's write this out for fun ...7,000,000,000,000,000,000,000,000,000 atoms.

If you were to remove all of the empty space contained in every atom in every person on planet Earth and compress us all together, then the overall volume of our atoms would be **less than a sugar cube!** Is that not extraordinary? You may be wondering what that sugar cube would weigh?

Well, I can tell you that it would be incredibly dense. Those atoms are packed in very tightly. The weight would be 500 billion kilograms (1.1 trillion pounds)! That equates to about 100 million African Elephants or a medium sized mountain all contained in a sugar cube.

If you were to remove all the empty space of everything on the surface of the Earth like animals, humans, trees, all buildings, all infrastructure, all loose rocks and surface materials and compress all that together by removing the empty space between atoms. You would get an object about the size of a suitcase. It would weigh 20 quadrillion kilograms (44 quadrillion pounds)!

Based on this science we are forced to say that when we look out at the world around us, that there is nothing really there. **It is mainly empty space** despite appearances. What we think are solid objects and solid people are just illusions. We can look at a solid oak tree but when we look very, very, closely we find it is all empty space. It is the same with everything. Concrete buildings, aeroplanes, trucks are all empty space when we look closely enough. It is extraordinary and when scientists first discovered this, it was quite a surprise too.

Does this discovery fit in with hypothesis that we are living in a computer game? The answer is yes. This is exactly what we would expect in a particular type of computer game. A holographic one. It is highly likely that the computer game we are playing in, is in the form of a hologram. **This means that everything around us is a holographic projection.** When I say everything is a hologram, I mean everything, including you. You, just like everything else in the universe are just a hologram.

This is quite a radical idea. **You are a hologram**. A lot of people will resist this idea strongly, but it is the truth. Everything is a hologram. The person you think you are may be a hologram but there is something in you that is real and that is your soul. You have a soul. As I mentioned earlier, more correctly you are a soul. This soul is made of divine consciousness. When your body dies your soul continues to live because it is immortal. It will re-join with your higher self in the spirit world. The higher self is your true identity not the body you are now. To become enlightened, you need to believe this. If you continue to think you are the body and mind you have now, then you will never become enlightened. I explain this in more detail later in this book.

Everything in this game seems so solid and real. It's so easy to forget that everything is mainly empty space. When source designed the multiverse, she did an outstanding job. It is so believable. If you climb a tree, it certainly doesn't feel like the tree is 99.9999999999996% empty space. If you fall from the tree, again it doesn't feel like your body is also almost all empty space. You are going to feel some pain when you hit the ground. The great Albert Einstein once said, "reality is merely an illusion, albeit a very persistent one." This is the thing; it feels so very real but it's not. It is just an incredible holographic simulation. It is not real at all. There is a passage in the Bible that hints at this. It is Luke 17:21 where Jesus said "for, behold, the kingdom of God is within you."

This quote hints at the truth that the code of the entire universe is written into your DNA. In a hologram the information of the whole hologram is encoded into every part of the hologram. Our human bodies are just a small part of the whole holographic universe but because of this principal of the whole being contained in every part, it means our bodies contain the information of our entire universe.

As well as that your personal peace, joy and happiness are also within you. If you are a spiritual seeker you don't need to go on a spiritual journey to India or the like. Heaven is not in a distant land somewhere. It is within you. Whenever you look within you are getting to know yourself a little more. Don't look for peace and happiness outside of yourself because it is not there. It is not at Lourdes, and it is not at Santiago. I'm not saying don't go on a pilgrimage to these places or anywhere else because that could be of benefit, but you don't need to do these things. Developing a habit of introspection and getting to know yourself by looking within will be of far greater benefit than any journey you might undertake.

Quantum physics explains to us that all form is empty space. The eastern religions tell us all form is empty. **Science and spirituality come together here in this book; reality is holographic.** If you accept this premise that reality is holographic you can see how this fits in perfectly with both science and spirituality.

Spooky action at a distance

There is a phenomenon in the universe known as quantum entanglement which baffles the brightest minds in physics. It is a phenomenon which is quite weird. It's about how two subatomic particles can become entangled with each other. Subatomic particles are the very tiny building blocks of the universe. They are tiny fragments which make up everything in the game. For example, a building is made up of tiny atoms and these atoms are made up of even tinier particles. Everything is made up of subatomic particles. Sometimes two particles can become linked or entangled together. This is not the baffling part. The baffling part is that if you separate these two particles, they remain linked together somehow. In fact, you could take one of the entangled particles and move it 5,000 kilometres from the other entangled particle. Despite this large distance separating them, they will remain in perfect communication with each other. Not only will the communication be perfect, it will also be instant.

If you were to interact with the first particle, what can happen is that the particle will demonstrate something which is known as spin. This spin will be either down spin or up spin. If the particle showed up spin say, the other particle which is 5,000 kilometres away will instantly exhibit down spin at the exact same moment despite being 5000 kilometres away.

In fact, you could take one entangled particle from a pair and move it to the edge of the observable universe and the two particles will even then, still remain in instant communication with each other. If the first particle shows spin up then the other particle at the edge of the universe will spin down, at the exact same instant. Einstein explained to us that nothing can travel faster than the speed of light. Yet, information between entangled particles most certainly does seem to travel faster than the speed of light. Einstein didn't like this proposition. He coined a phrase to describe this phenomenon, he called it "spooky action at a distance."

Many physicists have tried to understand quantum entanglement and spooky action at a distance but have ended up having to put it into the too hard basket. No one has been able to correctly explain how this information can travel faster than the speed of light. How can these particles remain linked together when they are literally billions of light years apart?

There is only one answer that I am aware of. It is because we are living in a holographic computer simulation. **The communication between entangled particles is simply part of the computer programming.** This solves this head scratcher straight away.

Quantum physics - the double slit experiment

Everyone in the world should know about the double slit experiment. This is the most famous physics experiment ever performed. The results of this experiment are jaw dropping. The double slit experiment has been performed over and over again and it always delivers the same astonishing result.

In this experiment subatomic particles like electrons are fired out of a device towards a barrier which has two vertical slits in it for the electrons to go through. Behind the barrier is a screen. The first time this experiment was conducted physicists expected to see the electrons go straight through the slits in the barrier and form two vertical lines on the screen directly behind the barrier. To their surprise this did not happen. Instead of two vertical lines on the screen the electrons formed the type of pattern you would expect to see if waves not particles had gone through the slits.

It was clear that the electrons were behaving as waves. To study this further, the physicists installed some cameras next to the slits to look closely at what was happening. A very strange thing then happened. It was as if the electrons knew they were being watched. After the installation of the cameras the pattern on the screen behind the barrier was different it showed two straight vertical lines. The electrons were no longer behaving like waves, they were behaving like particles now that they were being observed.

It was if the electrons were self-aware and changed their state once they knew they were being observed. This was an astonishing finding. At first the physicists couldn't believe what was happening. They repeated the experiment several times to be sure. Each time when the electrons were being observed they performed like particles and every time they were not observed they performed like waves.

One group of physicists tried something a little different. They put their cameras on the other side of the barrier after the electrons had already gone through the slits. To their surprise they got the same results. It was as if the electrons realised they were being observed and went back in time and went through the slits as particles rather than waves.

It is clear from this experiment that the stuff that makes up the world around us (subatomic particles) are self-aware. They know when they are being observed. If you happen to look down at a flower in your garden, that flower knows you are looking at it because that flower is self-aware. This is because a flower like everything else in the multiverse is made of subatomic particles just like the ones in the double split experiment. It is more alive and aware than anyone had imagined. This is quite extraordinary however it's not just flowers. Everything around us is made of atoms and each atom is made of subatomic particles. This means that quite literally everything is self-aware. Anything you can think of; clothes, cars, computers, water, rocks, factories, you name it, absolutely everything.

Remember, earlier in the book I said that everything is made of God stuff from the big bang. This means that everything is not only self-aware, everything is divine. Everything is God. There is only one God so this means everything is also one. To become enlightened, you need to see the world in this way. Because this is what reality is. It means you need to change your perspective so that you are aware of the truth. This universe we are a part of is incredibly dynamic. It is not just static and unchanging like most of us believed. **The fact that everything is God makes it more believable that everything is also self-aware.**

We will now continue to look at this remarkable fact that everything in our universe from rocks to human beings are completely self-aware.

Wave/particle duality

What does all this mean? It shows us that **any subatomic particle like an electron or any other subatomic particle exists as both a wave and a particle. This is known as wave/particle duality.**

If the subatomic particle is not being observed, it exists as a wave. What is the wave exactly? The wave is like a wave of probability or potentiality. The electron (or any other subatomic particle) is said to be in a super position. Think of it like the electron is in multiple positions at once, each with a probability attached to it.

The act of observation causes the wave to collapse to a single point based on these probabilities. Some positions have higher probabilities than others. The higher the probability the more likelihood that the electron will collapse to that point. An electron will collapse to one point only. An important point to understand is that you never know what position or point a wave will collapse into until after it has happened. Remember the collapse from a wave to a particle happens once it has been observed. It is impossible to predict which point the wave will collapse to until after the observation has taken place. **Before then all we can go on is probability.**

Why does it matter what position the wave will collapse to after it has been observed? **The position the electron (or other subatomic particle) collapses to determines what we see with our eyes when we look at it.**

This is quite incredible stuff. Have you worked out what all this means? It means that if no one is looking or observing something in the world around us then it is not actually there. It is existing as simply a wave of probability or potentiality. **For anything to appear and seem real we need a conscious observer to actually be there observing it.** If a conscious observer is looking at something then that something will appear, if no conscious observer is looking then there is nothing there at all except a wave of probability and potentiality.

Let's stick with the flower example. Remember a flower like everything else is made of subatomic particles. When we observe a flower, the waves that make up the flower collapse to a certain point based on probability (yes, there is an element of chance involved) and that determines what we see. If the wave collapses to one particular point we might see the flower looking at its best, healthy, brightly coloured and standing upright. If the wave collapses to a different point (perhaps a point with a lower probability) we might see a dead flower which has lost its colour and is not standing upright anymore.

Let's have another more complex example. Let's say you walk out of your house to jump in your car to go for a drive. Before you observe your car, it is existing as a wave of probability or potentiality (it is not really there). This is because it is made of subatomic particles and no conscious observer is observing it. As soon as the car comes into your field of vision, the subatomic particles collapse from a wave into a particle in a specific place or point. **They collapse to a particle in a specific place or point based on probability.** They do this because they are self-aware and realise they are now being observed by a conscious observer.

The place or point they collapse to determines what you see with your eyes when the car comes into your vision. Remember that they collapse based on probability. So, what do you see? 99% of the time the car will probably look much the same with subtle differences like different amounts of dirt on the car. Depending on the probabilities playing out there could be all sorts of different things that could pop up e.g., dirty windows, bird droppings or scratches on the panels. You could even find that you have a flat tyre, although this would have a low probability.

This is how the game works. I realise that this may seem almost unbelievable to a lot of people, but this is based on science. **It has been scientifically proven over and over again that subatomic particles know when they are being observed and that the act of observation itself causes the subatomic particles to collapse from a wave to a specific point or place based on probability.**

Most double slit experiments are carried out in laboratories. But what if we tried something more interesting. What if we studied the light coming from a distant galaxy? Particles of light are called photons. Photons are also a subatomic particle. So, light should in theory behave the same way as electrons. This has been studied. Scientists have put the light (photons) that has come from a far-away galaxy and put it through two slits as in the double slit experiment. What they observed on the screen behind the slits was a wave like pattern. This tells us that the light (photons) from the distant galaxy which has been travelling for billions of years has travelled the entire way as a wave of potentiality or probability. The next thing they did was install observational detectors to look at the photons closeup. Just like with the lab experiments as soon as the detectors were installed the photons collapsed from a wave of potentiality into specific particles and showed up as two straight lines on the screen. Here is the amazing part of this. The wave collapsed all the way back to the source of the light. All the way back to the distant galaxy billions of light years away on the other side of the universe!

This is called retro causality, where the particles reach back in time and alter their state. The important thing to understand is that they only do this if they are being observed. So, it seems that all the stars and galaxies out there exist only as projections and only become more detailed if we get up close. This is just the way a computer game works. A computer game only shows a simple projection of any part of the game which is not being interacted with. This is because it's the best way to save on computing power. There's no reason to show all the detail if no one is looking. It seems to work this way for both computer games and what we consider real life. If someone does suddenly start looking very closely at light from a far-away galaxy, then a collapse will occur instantly without you noticing and you will be able to see everything in detail as though it had been like that the whole time. Is this not absolutely extraordinary?

It is the same with the flower and the car. If there is no conscious observer looking at these two things, then why waste computer power by making them appear real. There are so many different things on our planet. **This simulation we are in saves a lot of computer power by not showing these things until a conscious observer happens to be looking directly at them. Computer games work in exactly the same way. Is this just a co-incidence? Or is it more proof that the world around us is actually a computer simulation?**

It is not there if you are not looking

What implications does this double slit experiment have for our lives? It holds massive implications. Remember that everything around us is made up of atoms which are made up of subatomic particles. This means if we happen not to be observing something and no other conscious observer is either, then it does not exist as we think it does. It exists in multiple states at once as described by the wave of super position and potentiality.

This is quite an extraordinary thing to say so let's say it another way:

If no one is looking at something, then it is not there. It is only existing as a wave of potentiality all based on probabilities.

To many this all sounds pretty far-fetched. You may be thinking this is crazy talk. However, this theory has the backing of a Nobel Prize behind it. The Nobel Prize for Physics in 2022 went to a group of scientists who proved that "the universe is not locally real." The winners of the award were Alain Aspect, John F Clauser and Anton Zellinger. Real, in this sense means that objects have definite properties independent of observation. These three scientists received the Nobel Prize for proving that this is not true. **Objects only become real when they are observed.**

Let's have another example. This means that if you have a tree house for your kids in your back yard, it does not exist unless a conscious observer is right there looking at it. Just like the previous examples of the flower and the car. What an amazing claim. This doesn't seem to make sense unless of course we are living in a holographic computer game. Then it makes perfect sense. Because that is how computer games work. Computer games only show that part of the game that the player is up too and interacting with. They don't show every part of the game at once as this is a waste of computing power. If you are up to level 2 say of a computer game, then the computer doesn't need to calculate everything necessary for level 1 or level 3. It will just show you level 2.

In the same way if you are in your backyard. You will see the tree house. Your will see it in detail because you are a conscious observer right there looking at it but at the same moment your bedroom inside the house has ceased to exist. Why? Because no one is observing it. It will exist only as a wave of potentiality to save on computing power. When you walk back inside your house and into your bedroom the wave will collapse, and you will see the bedroom in detail. At this point the tree house has gone back to existing as a wave of potentiality all based on probabilities. Everything seems continuous for the observer; you don't notice any of this happening. It turns out our world is far more dynamic than most people realise. Every single object or piece of nature does not exist unless there is a conscious observer right there looking at it. Everything pops in and out of existence depending on whether it is being observed. One must be prepared to really open their mind to know the truth. Are you prepared to open your mind enough to believe this?

Now you can see why the double slit experiment is the most incredible experiment ever performed. It tells us the answer to the age-old question; does a tree that falls in the woods make a noise if no one is there to hear it? The answer is that without a conscious observer the tree itself does not even exist. The whole tree is existing as a wave of potentiality with probabilities attached to it. One of these probabilities is that the tree will fall over. But if there is no conscious observer then this event cannot happen. If someone was to go to the woods and walk up to the spot where the tree is they will cause a collapse of the wave of potentiality and they will most likely either see the tree on the ground or still standing (depending on the probabilities playing out). Either way the tree has not made a noise. The only way it could make a noise is if it fell over at the exact moment the conscious observer arrived at the tree, but this would have a very low probability of happening.

A simulation of the multiverse would require a massive amount of processing power. It may require harnessing all the energy and power of an entire star. So, it makes perfect sense that the computer creating this multiverse would only compute those parts of the game which are being interacted with. It is important to understand that this happens in an instant. We don't even notice. From our point of view everything seems set and solid with no change. This is a quite an amazing thing to behold. We live in a dynamic game which is constantly appearing and disappearing all according to probabilities.

Consciousness is the operating system and belief is the language

In Chapter 1 we explained that everything in the game is made of consciousness. These building blocks of everything around us are alive and self-aware. In other words, they know when they are being observed. We can now say that consciousness is the operating system of the game we are playing. Now that we know everyday objects appear and disappear depending on whether they are being observed or not, it suddenly makes sense that everything is made of consciousness. It suddenly makes sense that everyday objects know when they are being observed. It suddenly makes sense that consciousness and not spacetime is the fundamental reality of the game. Objects know when they are being observed by a conscious observer because they are made of consciousness itself. They are alive. They are divine. They are God.

If consciousness is the operating system of the game, then the language of the game is belief. **Belief helps determines which specific outcome will result from the collapse of the wave of potentiality**. The higher our belief of a specific outcome, the higher the probability that that outcome will be realised. So now we have two things that will determine what we see when we observe something. Firstly, there is an aspect of luck as explained in the previous section but as well as this your belief plays a role. In the next section we will learn that there is a third factor which determines what we see and experience in the universe. That is God or source's divine will.

Because we now know that source is creating with you, I will now use the term **co-creating** when explaining the process of creation. Using the word co-creating is much more accurate because you do have source working with you in the creation process. But for now, let us examine the second factor which determines your results in life- that is your personal belief.

Let's have an example of the power of belief in creating what you experience in the game. Let's look at Tracy who has an apple tree in her back yard. She feels hungry and wonders to herself if there may be any ripe apples on the tree for her to eat. So, she goes outside to check. In her mind she thinks there will most likely be three apples that are ripe enough to pick. This is her belief. The game of life gives her what she believes. So, when she walks into the garden and checks for apples the most probable outcome is that she will find exactly three apples. The next most probable outcome is either 2 or 4 apples. Finding say 7 apples has a lower probability and finding 15 has a very low probability but is still possible.

The game is very dynamic. Our belief is the key language that determines all the results we get in life but there is still some luck attached to everything because of the probabilities playing out. **As well as belief and luck, we must remember we are co-creating with source (divine will) so it's not all just down 100% to our beliefs and luck it is a joint process**. So, in the apple example, Tracy could find 20 ripe apples, it's just that this outcome is much less likely. The key thing to understand is that a lot of it comes down to Tracy's belief. If she had believed that there would probably be no apples at all and that most of the apples would be affected by disease, then it is a whole different ball game. All the probabilities would be different, and her results would be different.

This process of co-creating our life is mainly done by the subconscious mind. If you have a closed mind, you will not co-create as many interesting things in your life compared to someone with an open mind. I ask you to open your mind both consciously and subconsciously. If you expect miracles, then you will get miracles. If you believe nothing interesting ever happens to you then that is what you will get.

A fun thing to do is to ask your angels or spirit guides to give you a surprise then keep an open mind and wait for it to come. The more you believe interesting and enjoyable things will happen to you, the more it will. You are playing this game co-creating with source your life around you. You have been doing this since the moment you were born. It is just that you didn't realise it because it is the subconscious mind which has been doing most of the co-creating. Can you see just how powerful you are? You are literally God walking this Earth co-creating everything around you as you go. The only prerequisite is that you believe. So, open your mind and start believing in miracles. Start believing that fun, interesting and stimulating things happen to you daily. Then sit back and enjoy playing this game.

Most people believe the world is set and static remaining much the same from moment to moment. What I am describing here is a very different world. I am describing a world of constant change where new realities just emerge responding to people's subconscious minds. 8 billion people literally creating the world around us. The game is totally dynamic. It is the ultimate computer game.

We are co-creating our lives

We now know that we are co-creating our life with our beliefs. What is happening to us in this game is not just random. We are not just victims of fate. We are at cause in terms of our life. This is a radical philosophy. It means we can't really blame anyone else for things we think have gone wrong in our life.

I am describing a radical and very dynamic game, where a combination of belief and luck and divine will seems to determine the results we get in life. This applies to everything that happens in this game not just picking apples from trees as in the example earlier.

Some people reading this may be experiencing a strong negative reaction to the idea we are co-creating our life with our beliefs. You may have a serious illness or have experienced the loss of loved ones. You will be thinking that you most certainly did not co-create that and why would you co-create such awful outcomes. One must remember that the divine will of source is a big part of the creation process. We are co-creating our life with source. It is not 100% all down to our beliefs and luck. Sometimes source has a different plan for us than what we want. She knows what is best and she may use her creative powers to make something happen that we don't want at all. We must always keep in mind that source is working from a divine blueprint, and she knows what is best for us. We cannot control divine will. Source knows what is best for our life and she will control part of our life. We can only control what we can control. All we can do is control our beliefs by being positive and then give up or surrender the rest to the divine will of source.

People who are very negative seem to get very negative results in their life. They get what they believe. Other people who always expect the best generally get exactly that. It can be easy to get trapped in a negative thought-outcome loop. Each negative outcome just reinforces the negative thinking, and the negative thinking keeps creating negative outcomes. It can be difficult to break this cycle if it is really entrenched. Often if you try to turn this around by being super positive, things may actually get worse before they get better. This is analogous to a dirty sink in your kitchen. There may be lots of dirt and grime there. You decide to clean it up with water and detergent. When you start scrubbing for a while the sink gets even more messy. It takes a bit of time before you have got the sink nice and clean. It's the same in this game. If you have been a negative person for a long time and suddenly you decide to change and be super positive, your life may get messier for a while before it gets better. You must just keep up the positive beliefs and hang in there until it does turn around.

You have already co-created some incredible things in your life without even knowing you were co-creating these things. Imagine now what lies ahead. Now that you know you are literally God playing a game that you created for yourself, imagine what might happen in the future. By opening your mind anything could happen. Life will respond to you. You co-create with your beliefs so the more things you believe could be possible the more interesting and enjoyable things you can co-create. Why not believe that you are going to live a life where every day is an adventure. Where you are constantly surprised and stimulated. It is your call. You can make this happen. You are co-creating with source, so if you do this source will come to the party by giving you experiences in life that are tuned in to your beliefs of what is possible. I want to add a very important proviso. If source does not want you to create something then you won't create it. Strictly speaking from a pure non-dual perspective there is no co-creation because everything is one. Your soul and source are one. So there is only one creator which is Source. This is from a very high level non-dual perspective. Here in this book I make a concession and teach co-creation by the soul and source. I do this because it is more useful to the reader and the level of spiritual understanding most readers have.

The creation process is only possible in a computer game

This description of our world seems incredible. We are talking about a game which is conscious and self-aware and can even know what our beliefs are and then give us that. This is extraordinary. How could this be? Because life is a holographic computer game, that's why. It is only possible for this to happen if we were in a computer game. There is no other way. When you accept the fact that we are living in a computer game, then you can suddenly see how the conscious world around us responds to our beliefs. This happens because it is part of the programming. It is that simple. This is the nature of the game. This is how the game works.

Creating our life in a cold, materialistic universe is unlikely but creating our life in a holographic computer game makes perfect sense.

Some people may say that life is just so complex and nuanced how could it possibly be a computer simulation. Yes, life is incredibly complex and nuanced and there is an enormous number of things happening. The answer to this objection is that we simply are too primitive to understand how it is possible. Source is so much more advanced than us we can hardly measure it. We don't have the brain power to understand how this could be. It is beyond us. Consider a pet cat. It knows that each day at roughly the same time it gets fed but it knows nothing about what we as players need to do to get the money to supply the cat food. It is beyond the cat's intelligence to ever know. We are the same with God. Heaven knows how this computer simulation was designed all we know is that we are a part of it.

It is now clear that for this process to work properly, we must have a conscious observer. It is the act of observation that collapses the wave. What happens when different observers with different beliefs observe the same thing? This is an excellent question that had me stumped for quite a while. It was only after I learned about the quantum physics interpretation known as "Many Worlds Theory," that I was able to piece this together. To answer this question above, let's now learn about the Many Worlds interpretation of quantum physics.

Many worlds interpretation

This interpretation of quantum physics in very simple terms, states that at each moment when a decision is made, the universe splits and that all possible outcomes are realised in another "world" or universe.

This implies that every possible outcome or situation you could possibly think of does exist in a parallel universe. So, for example, there is a universe where you are President of the United States of America. It's important to realise that this universe where you are the President of the United States of America is just as real as this game you are playing now. It does have an extremely low probability attached to it, however. But nevertheless, it certainly still does exist.

Many worlds can be thought of as a many branched tree where every possible outcome is realised. Many physicists believe that there are an infinite number of parallel worlds or universes. Once again, the multiverse splits whenever a decision is made, and every possible outcome is realised in one particular universe.

So, returning to the question of what happens when different observers with different beliefs observe the same thing. In these situations, each observer will get what they believe by splintering off into the reality that reflects that belief. Because there are infinite parallel universes all beliefs can be accommodated.

Choosing to exist in a specific splinter of reality

Let's have an example of athletes about to run the race of their lives, the Olympic women's 100 metre final. There are eight women about to contest the final. We have learnt that results in life come from belief. This tells us that these women must have had enough belief in themselves to make this final. You may be thinking that it's not about belief but more about natural ability and the training they have done. Of course, this is true. These are huge factors, but belief works alongside these factors. In a race like this it is belief that gives you that extra bit that makes all the difference. Ask any top-level athlete and they will tell you, that you can't win if you don't believe you can win.

It is the combination of performance and belief which will determine the result of this race. Let's say Abigay from Jamaica wins the final by .12 of a second from the American athlete Tina. It was Abigay's very fast start out of the blocks that was decisive. Conversely, Tina was a little slow out of the blocks and couldn't peg Abigay back. Was that fast start by Abigay skill, or was there some luck involved with her timing being so spot on? Most people would say a bit of both. Again, any top athlete will tell you that you need a bit of luck to win. But is it really luck that Abigay started so well or was it her belief that she would win. Abigay won the gold medal because she had so much belief, that the universe was forced into aligning perfectly for her. It was her belief that allowed her to anticipate the starters gun to the microsecond and get that early lead over the rest of the field.

You might say, well what if the American athlete Tina also believed she could win the gold medal. Then it becomes a matter of who believes the most. Whose combination of ability, performance and belief is the greatest. Remember that the "Many Worlds" interpretation of quantum physics states that all possible outcomes are realised in another "world" or universe. This means that in another parallel universe Tina won the gold medal. In this universe she had more belief and performed better. **Maybe both of these two athletes won at the same time.** It may be that Tina simply splintered off to a different universe where she was the winner. There are also parallel universes where each of the other 6 athletes had superior belief and won too. Each of these parallel universes being just as real as Abigay's win.

In this way each player in the game is constantly taking different branches of the tree of life. Constantly splintering to different realities.

Success comes from belief

I have been a music lover since I was about 10 years old. I enjoy the genre of music known as alternative rock or indie pop/rock. My two favourite bands of all time have both produced some stunning creative music but had very different levels of success in terms of record sales. The first band "The Smiths" out of Manchester, England took the music world by storm in the 1980's. Their front man Morrissey is known as being a lyrical genius. Their music was different to anything I had ever heard before. Aching melodies and creative lyrics along with the charismatic Morrisey propelled them to huge success and cemented their spot in history. They still have a very large and loyal tribe of fans today. Morrisey is an incredibly talented man who used his music to speak to his listeners about social issues such as veganism.

My other favourite band of all time is "The Go-Betweens," this band formed in Brisbane Australia in the early 1980's before moving to London England in the hopes of finding fame. They too had a distinctive style of music. With lots of melancholy in their sound their music was very good. But for some reason they were never able to crack the big time and find commercial success. They certainly had the talent and their songs as I have mentioned were creative and original. Like the Smiths, even today they have a loyal group of fans and a cult like following. There was charisma in this band too. One of the lead singers was Robert Forster and he always looked the part with his dress sense and heavy makeup.

But why were the Smiths able to succeed commercially and the Go-Betweens could not. Was it simply a case of the Smiths being much better? I don't think so. I think it came down to belief. Morrissey has been quoted as saying that he was not surprised when The Smiths took off. He has said that he expected success all along. I think that is the key. We get what we expect, and The Smiths always believed they could make it big. On the other hand, The Go-Betweens simply didn't believe enough. For whatever reasons consciously and subconsciously they believed they would never crack the big time in the music world. So, like everyone they got what they believed.

Just like with the Olympic women's 100 metre final, there are other realities where The Go-Betweens managed to become one of the biggest bands in the world. These splinters of reality are just as real as this reality

How far will belief take you? How big are the things you can manifest?

We have now learnt that we can co-create our life with our thoughts and beliefs. We now know we are literally God walking around, subconsciously (mainly) co-creating life all around us. Many people believe they can manifest a broad range of things playing this game. But to what extent is this possible? Do you believe you could manifest a perfect doctor's appointment at just the right time for example? What about something more difficult like manifesting a promotion at work? Everyone has a line they subconsciously draw somewhere. At which point does it become too much to manifest. To be honest, the majority of the world's population don't believe that they can manifest anything at all. What do you believe? Where do you draw the line?

Belief is a mixture of the power of both the conscious and subconscious minds. A lot of the time it is the subconscious which is the most powerful creative force. The subconscious process in the appendix of this book will help you clear away blocks you have in your subconscious mind which are blocking your ability to manifest big things in your life. Here is a quote from the Bible attributed to Jesus:

"Truly I tell you, if you have faith as small as a mustard seed, you can say to this mountain, 'move from here to there,' and it will move. Nothing will be impossible for you." **Matthew 17:20-21.**

Faith and belief in this context are essentially the same thing. Jesus is telling us we can literally move mountains if we believed enough. "Nothing will be impossible for you." I believe every word of this. Why is it that many people believe they can manifest small things in life but consider many other things impossible? The reason is they are thinking small but moreover they have no idea of just how powerful they are as creators.

The power of one

I strongly believe that as individuals we can co-create anything. There is nothing we can't do. What I am about to say is something I have seen very few spiritual teacher's say. This has always surprised me. Here it is...

You have the power as an individual to manifest or change significant worldwide issues.

The problem of course is usually we don't have enough belief to do it. Here is an example. Do you believe you could do this on your own by force of belief?

Change the weather by breaking a drought.

You have enough creative power to do this just by yourself. That is an extraordinary thing to say but I stand by it. It is just a matter of belief. If your belief is strong enough, the game must respond by giving you what you believe. In the past indigenous Americans would perform rain dances to induce rain. They knew the power of belief. Mixing belief into a ceremony or a performance is a strong message to the universe. We are far more powerful than most people realise. Do you believe this? Do you believe you have the power as an individual to manifest or change significant worldwide issues? I ask you to keep an open mind. Many people believe they can manifest a perfect car park. Why not manifest drought breaking rain? This can seem quite easy when you compare this to moving an entire mountain like Jesus has said we can do.

Some people may say that there are billions of people on the planet so how could one person do something that affects everyone. The answer is because if you achieved this you are co-creating a splinter in the "Many Worlds" universe. You will go to that "world" that already exists where it is raining. If other people believe something different, then they won't go with you. They will stay in the "world" where there is no rain.

But I hear you say, I will still see everyone else in my new world so I must have brought them with me. Great question. The answer is no you haven't brought others with you. You will be joined in this new "world" by a different version of other people. That version of other people who mostly do believe (either consciously or subconsciously) that the drought is broken. Some people will be there just by default because the drought was not something they were focusing on. Just like the way some things happen to you that you weren't focused on. However, these other people will still appear to be the same people. You will not notice any difference at all. They will have exactly the same memories, but they are a different version when it comes to this weather event you have manifested. Remember that if there are infinite universes in this game that means there are infinite versions of you and everybody else.

The Truman Show

Each soul is at the centre of their very own universe, or we could say, at the centre of their very own extraordinary game. So, each soul is a game in their own right. We go about co-creating everything around us and we are at the very centre of this creative power. We all do this and we kind of overlap with other souls who are at the centre of their games too. Each soul co-creating an entire world around them and this all blends together because there are so many parallel universes to accommodate this blending.

Have you seen the movie The Truman Show? In this movie a man's entire life is a TV show. The TV show is all centred on him.

Your life is similar. I'm not saying that your life is a TV show, but I am saying that everything that happens in life is centred around you. Remember you are playing a game here. You are the number one player and everyone else are just extras in this extraordinary game. Synchronicities that occur are all occurring just for you. It is almost as if you are the only person in the world. Everything that happens in life is happening for you. There are signs from the divine which are for you to pick up on. Messages, synchronicities all designed to specifically help you in your game. Almost as if everyone else are just like the actors on The Truman Show. This is the way the game works for everyone. Because there are infinite parallel universes everyone can be at the very centre of their very own game.

This is analogous to a dream we might have when we are asleep. The subconscious mind creates the entire dream and all the characters but localises itself as one character, you. **You are at the very centre of your dream and all the other characters are just like extras.** Waking life is very similar to the dream state. If you can create an entire world in your dreams, then you can co-create a world in this holographic computer simulation.

Creation from fear

There is another thing to consider. I have explained that belief is the language of the computer game we are playing in. Belief is the most powerful creative force. However, it is not the only creative force. Sometimes there are other feelings or emotions which co-create the world around us. One of these is fear. If we fear something happening, then that which we fear may well happen.

Can you think of examples in your life where this might have occurred? There is a person I met many years ago who has always had a fear that she would not be able to find a life partner. She had many casual sexual partners throughout her teens and twenties but no real lasting relationship. Eventually though, she met someone and formed a relationship. The relationship was going so well that she became engaged. Unfortunately for her this person broke off the engagement and the relationship ended. Fast forward three decades later and she has been living alone for a very long time. This story is hardly unique. Many people have experienced this exact same situation.

I used to think that if we feared something we would then take-action to ensure that that thing we feared would not happen. This was very naïve of me. If we are thinking about being alone as in this example, then we obviously have this fear in our mind. We are repeatably thinking about it, day in day out, over and over. This is what does the damage. Just the sheer amount of attention we are bringing to it. What happens is we think about being alone so much that we splice off into a version of the game where indeed we are alone with no romantic partner.

This lady in my example above let herself go after the engagement broke off. She put on a lot of weight. She drinks heavily and she smokes cigarettes. She has actually made herself unappealing as a romantic partner. All of this stems from the root fear of never finding lasting love. This shows how behaviours can have their genesis in limiting beliefs and negative emotions. In the appendix of this book I have a process you can do to remove these types of limiting beliefs and negative emotions.

This occurs to not just life partners. What is it that you fear? Be honest with yourself. Is the thing you fear actually holding you back in your life? If so, then you need to change the script. Firstly, use the subconscious process in the appendix of this book to clear this fear from your subconscious mind. Then use the law of attraction as explained in Chapter 1 to manifest what it is that you do want. When we do this, we are moving from being a passive participant in life to being a conscious creator.

Another example of a person creating through fear is a person I watch regularly on YouTube. I will call him Tom. Tom plays table games at a Las Vegas casino and streams them live every day. He mainly plays ultimate Texas hold'em poker and blackjack. I have been watching him for nearly a year at this time of writing. I have found to my surprise that I enjoy watching others play table games at casinos. I find myself rooting for them to win.

Almost every session that Tom plays, he is complaining. He complains about his bad luck. He doesn't just say it once he says it over and over again.

He is on repeat right through the entirety of most videos. He believes that he has the worst luck out of anyone in the world and this is what he says almost every day in his videos. He says that no one in the entire world gets as much bad luck as he does. He tells us that he gets the statistical minimum back on his bets. He mentions that he hopes to one day have no luck (yes, no luck) because he says no luck would be far better than what he gets now. He really does believe what he says. He really does believe he is the unluckiest gambler in the world. He is a very nice guy and very likeable, but he is very negative with his words.

When you watch his videos, it does seem like he has incredibly rotten luck. I have never seen any player get as many losing hands as he does. He seems to always find a way to lose a hand. Everything he tries to do seems to somehow backfire on him. He certainly loses a lot more than he wins. Quite simply, luck is rarely on his side.

What he doesn't realise is that he is creating bad luck through his negativity. He plays in a very fearful way and he expects bad cards to come up and make him lose. He is creating bad luck through his fear and his constant negative commentary which is on repeat. Over and over he is describing how horrific his luck is. He is telling the universe over and over that he is the unluckiest gambler in the world. So, what do you think happens? The universe gives him what he expects. He expects to lose so the universe makes him lose.

In this example it is partly Tom's negative words which create the bad luck. But it's his emotions too. His emotions do the real damage. It is fear for sure but other emotions as well. Often, he is frustrated or angry, sometimes he is exasperated. His negative words are powered up with his negative emotions so that the universe gives him exactly what he believes to be true.

You might say that the cards are set in a specific order and nothing can change that. Playing cards involves a lot of luck however. Do you play one hand or two? Do you take another card or not? Do you split? Do you double? Do you fold or take a risk? These are decisions that Tom must make, and they determine whether he wins or loses. He almost always seems to make the wrong decisions and thus he loses. He is choosing to splinter off into the reality which already exists in the game where he makes the wrong decision and loses.

Everyone who plays games at casinos will lose in the long run because the house has a statistical advantage. It is just that Tom loses much faster than most people do. A perfect example of creating through fear and negative belief.

Don't think you can believe your way to win at gambling long term. You may think you can be the opposite of Tom and believe you can beat the casino. You won't because the casino has a statistical advantage which will beat you. You won't be able to keep up the belief that you are going to win. The losses will pile up and you won't believe anymore. There are some things like this that simply won't happen even if you believe. This is because this computer simulation simply can't support a delusional belief. For example, you may believe you can fly and you jump off a building. You are going to go splat if you do this. There are limits to what you can create through belief and also through fear.

Seeing everything in life through the prism of wealth

Whether we know it or not we are already co-creating our life and have been since the day we were born. It is just that most people don't realise that they have been doing it. They are co-creating by default. Think of the massive mix of different thoughts, desires, fears we have in our mind even just in one day. There is a real mixture of everything. That's why many people get mixed results. Imagine what life can be like if we exercise some control over the jumble of thoughts, feelings, and emotions we have. We can have coherent themes running through our conscious and subconscious minds.

Imagine if you decided to live a life where the main theme running through your life was **wealth**. A wealth of everything from **health to money**. Everything that happens to you in life you see it through the prism of wealth. Do this for ten years and you can guess what happens. You are a wealthy person. Let's look closer at this example. It does not mean you think you are wealthy, so you just spend lots of money using credit cards. Not at all. You adopt the qualities of wealthy people. For example, one of the richest people on the planet is Warren Buffett and he had a rule whereby for a very long time he lived on a highly restricted budget. He valued frugality. He chose to live within a restricted means even though he could have lived far more lavishly. He did this for a long time. For decades. To be precise he restricted himself to an annual income of US$100,000 and he did this for forty years. He is a billionaire, so if he wanted to he could have given himself much more money to live off. He didn't because he knew the power of exponential growth over time. He was thinking long term and he built himself a fortune.

A great trick you can use is to always have a $100 note in your wallet which you never touch or spend. This is very powerful because by doing this you are living this philosophy of feeling wealthy and living frugally at the same time. You may think what is the point of doing this. You could be amazed at how powerful this is. You will have a feeling of being wealthy and as you get by each day without touching it, it encourages you. You feel good because you know that you are doing it. You are living the philosophy of feeling wealthy and living frugally.

So, adopt the value of frugality and at the same time make sure you feel wealthy or feel abundance. You feel the feelings of being a wealthy person, but you don't spend like a rich person might. Get rid of most of your credit cards. It's a nice feeling to know you can afford the latest electronic device but at the same time choosing to not buy it. You can also become financially literate. Learn about how money grows exponentially when it is invested. Understand the power of compound growth and exponential returns. Become an expert on creating wealth. You will understand that if you take $100 and double it every year after ten years you will have over $100,000. After 15 years you will have over $3 million dollars. You will understand that if you halve your weekly alcohol budget you may be able to retire years earlier not to mention improve your general health.

If you are still young or young enough to be a decade or more away from giving up work. Adopt this motto; **have less now so that you can have much more later.** Compound interest (earning interest on interest) works so that the earlier you start saving the higher the returns are over time and the returns increase exponentially.

Adopt the habit of saving 10% of every dollar you earn and put this money aside. Leave it, don't spend a cent of it unless you want to buy an appreciating asset (an asset which goes up in value over time) like a house. If you do get to the point where you want to buy a house, don't do what many people do and that is buy the most expensive and best house they could possibly afford. Doing this could trap you into poverty because you will be so stretched trying to make the mortgage payments. This period of being financially stressed can last 30 years or more. Instead buy a good house but one you can easily afford so that you have enough money to enjoy life and do enjoyable things.

Even if all you are earning is a small amount of money from a part time job, make sure you save 10%. Do you realise that if you start saving 10% from age 18 you will create far more wealth than a person who started at

21? Those extra three years are super powerful. The exponential effect of those three years is crazy. Crazy in a good way!

Here is a scenario that will blow you away. Imagine you are a person who buys a cafe latte everyday paying around $5.50 for one large cup. Imagine if you decided to halve your coffee intake. You decide to buy coffee every second day instead. That will save you close to $1000 a year. Now invest that $1000 in a high interest saving account. Keep adding another $1000 every year that goes by (remember you are financing this from halving your coffee budget). After 20 years at 4% interest compounding you will have $27,172. After 40 years you will have $86,711. In actuality you will have even more money than this as inflation will increase the price of a cup of coffee over time. If we assume an inflation rate of 3% per year the total saved will be $35,132 after 20 years and $140,460 saved over 40 years. Wow! Just by halving the amount of coffee you buy, you will be $140,460 richer after 40 years!

What if you decided after 20 years to go back to buying coffee every day again and invest the $35,132 into an **investment property**? You now get the benefit of **leverage**. Let's say you bought this property for $351,320 (that's a 10% deposit coming from your coffee savings of $35,132). Property roughly doubles in value every 10 years. So, after another 20 years the value of your investment property would be **$1,405,280**. Is this not quite incredible? By simply halving the amount of coffee you buy for 20 years you have become a **millionaire** within 40 years!

I haven't even mentioned the regular rent money coming in. After twenty years that rent money would have increased a lot too and will provide you a passive income stream for your retirement. Think about this the next time you are getting a coffee from Starbucks!

This last example combines the two superpowers of investing; **compound interest and leverage** (gaining access to an asset of high value using a fraction of that amount of money- in this case 10%). When you combine the two you have the ability to create enormous wealth. All that is required is **sacrifice** (not buying a latte every day)**, discipline** (investing the coffee savings) **& patience** (letting time pass). This is not rocket science. Anyone can do this. Including you.

Actually my last couple of sentences are not entirely true. I said anyone can do this and that is false. The words just came out from my fingers on the keyboard before I remembered the reality of massive inequality in this world. There are many people who cannot afford to buy a latte even once a year. Those people living in deep poverty. For these people the future seems bleak. My advice for people in this situation is to use education to gain qualifications so they can enter the work force and have a chance at creating wealth in all areas of their life.

The reality though is that this is easier said than done especially if you are surrounded by domestic abuse or people with addictions. I don't have all the answers for these people but I just wanted to acknowledge that the financial strategies I am outlining here may be too far removed for some people. This needed to be said. However the potential for enlightenment **is** available to all. That is the focus of this book.

Having wealth, including financial wealth is a good thing. Some people may feel that being wealthy or simply that money itself is not very spiritual. For example take the vow that catholic priests, brothers and sisters take when they are ordained. A vow of poverty. I don't believe that this vow is very useful. Although the definition of poverty in the Catholic church is a loose term and most Catholic clergy live sparse but comfortable lives. They will never be rich but they will always be well fed and have a roof over their heads.

Even the Buddha himself tried this philosophy of poverty and self-denial of material assets and even food. The Budda realised eventually that this is not the way to go. He tried this method and he made no spiritual gains. He realised that the best course is what he called "the middle way." Basically this means being financially comfortable. Not too poor but not too rich either. I certainly agree with the Buddha. You don't need to be a billionaire. It's unlikely that you will attain enlightenment if you are living a life of pure luxury.

Having said that, money gives you freedom and there is nothing spiritual about being poor. It is better to have enough money in your life so that you are free enough to do more things and enjoy life. You will be able to support a charity and do good deeds with your money.

If you have limiting beliefs or "stuff" about money you can clear these subconscious limiting beliefs with my limiting belief blaster at the back of this book. Here are some typical limiting beliefs people have about money:

Money is not spiritual
Money is hard to come by
I don't deserve money
I am not good with money

Having money is selfish
You have to work hard for money
I never have enough money

Use the subconscious limiting belief blaster at the back of this book to erase these limiting beliefs from your subconscious mind. It only takes one minute to blast a belief. Then use the state saturation process which is also at the back of this book to saturate your body and your cells at the quantum level with this following state:

I am wealthy in all areas of my life

Make smart decisions with your spending. Your ego may want you to buy a flash car so that you might impress other people. The moment you drive that flash car off the lot, you lose thousands of dollars. You will most likely have borrowed money at high interest to pay for this car and the car is decreasing in value faster than your loan balance. People fall into this trap all the time. Who cares what others think of you? You might end up bankrupting yourself just because your ego wanted to impress others. Doing this can end up costing you many tens of thousands of dollars over the lifetime of the loan. You may as well dig a hole and bury your money. By the time you finally pay it off you might find that the amount would have been enough to put down as a deposit for a house (an appreciating asset). Why not just buy a good car that you can afford?

Another thing is you don't need to update your car every 5 or 6 years. You will lose a lot of money doing this. Why update if the car is driving well and getting you to where you need to go? Your ego wants you to update your car, but your ego is insecure and needs to look good, don't listen to it. Of course, if you have a lot of wealth and can afford to buy a nice car that makes your soul sing then by all means go ahead. But if you aren't at that place yet, I advise that you don't pretend you are.

If we do all these things I have mentioned in this section, what happens is we are consciously choosing to live in a particular splinter of reality where we are a wealthy person. Remember that this reality already exists. It is just that we are choosing to go into that reality. This process of picking and choosing realities or splintering off into different realities is happening all the time every day. We just can't see it. Everything is seamless but as I have already mentioned many physicists believe there are infinite parallel universes in this game. Nothing is impossible. If there is a reality where you are the King or Queen of England, then there is a reality where you are wealthy in all areas of your life and it's far more probable that being King or Queen of England.

Belief is the most powerful creative force. So, start believing and if you do this the universe must respond. It cannot do otherwise. It is a law of the universe.

We are living in a computer simulation. The reason I have written this section on wealth is because in built into the computer simulation is a program which allows you to manifest whatever you want in life. It is part of the programming of the simulation. It is a real law of the universe, and these financial tips above will help you manifest long term wealth. The key is to educate yourself about wealth building and put that into practice and at the same time you must **use your emotions to feel abundance.** That is how you co-create wealth.

The biggest synchronicity of them all

I would like to finish this chapter by mentioning some peculiarities in life which could be signs from a higher power that all is not quite as it seems. These peculiarities are pointing to something. I believe they are pointing to the truth that this life is a computer simulation. What's more this simulation is a game. A game we are all playing right now.

I have mentioned earlier that source gives us signs to pick up on in our lives. These signs are specifically for you to notice, and they often come in the form of synchronicities. Synchronicities are seeming coincidences but what is happening is actually not a coincidence at all. These seeming coincidences are messages coming from divine source.

There are small synchronicities and big ones. Every time we experience a total solar eclipse the universe is revealing to us the greatest synchronicity of them all. The synchronicity is that the Moon just happens to be the perfect size and the perfect distance to block out the Sun completely.

The Sun and the Moon are about the same size when you look at them in the sky. This is because the Sun is 400 times bigger than the Moon and also happens to be 400 times further away from us than the Moon. There is no reason that it has to be this way. It just is. Is this just a coincidence?

What this does mean is that we are lucky enough to see spectacular coronal displays during a total eclipse. What makes the odds of this happening even more unlikely is that we just happen to be alive at the right time for this to occur. In the Earth's past, the Moon was closer to the Earth so that it would have blocked out all the Sun plus more again. So, the cave people who were our ancestors would have missed out on seeing the stunning total eclipses that we see now. In the same way, if we were too fast forward 50,000 years into the future the Moon will be too far away to eclipse all the Sun.

In the grand scheme of the history of the Solar System 50,000 years is not a long time. So, it just happens that we are alive in the brief period of Earth's history where the Moon almost perfectly blocks the Sun.

I asked **AI** to calculate; what is the probability that a human incarnation and lifetime on Earth occurs during the brief window when total solar eclipses are possible? I am assuming that the Moon and the Earth could be any size and I am only calculating for the part of the universe's lifetime when life could theoretically arise. In other words a habitable stellar window or a life permitting epoch. I am also allowing for variability in the size of the Sun and variability in the distance from the Sun to the Earth (some assumptions were made in this calculation). The answer is that the probability of a total solar eclipse in your lifetime under these parameters is **.0000007743%. Which equates to one chance in 1.3 million!** That is a jaw dropping figure. Highly, highly unlikely!

That is not just rare, it's almost unimaginable and yet here we are alive to witness the Moon perfectly silhouetting the Sun, revealing its corona in a fleeting, celestial display. **It feels like a synchronicity written into the very architecture of the universe.**

Is this synchronicity trying to tell us something? Could it be that this is God's way of giving us a clue that **the universe is not real** and is in fact a computer simulation? Like all apparent synchronicities you can never prove this for sure, but it is interesting to ponder. I will leave it up to you to form your own opinion.

The Mandela Affect

The term "The Mandela Affect," has been coined because there is a large group of people who have false memories of this great man's life and of other pieces of history. The false memories of Nelson Mandela pertain to when he actually died. Nelson Mandela was released from prison on 11 February 1997, going on to become president of South Africa. He died on 4

December 2013. Yet there are hundreds of thousands of people who swear that they thought he died in prison in the 1980's. They specifically remember news broadcasts in the 1980's informing people of his death. The strange part of this is that so many strongly believe this. Could this be some sort of glitch in our computer game with many different versions of reality? Or could it be a deliberate sign from source?

There are many more examples of the Mandela Affect. Here are a few examples of false memories many people have which are not true at all. Did you believe some of these things? You are not alone if you do. There are many people who share these memories.

- Mother Teresa was made a saint in the 1980's. This never happened.
- The TV show Sex in the City. It was not called this. It was "Sex and the City."
- Snow White said "Mirror, Mirror on the Wall…" Again no, she did not say this. It was "Magic Mirror on the Wall…"
- The Monopoly man is remembered as wearing a monocle. In truth he didn't have a monocle.
- The country of New Zealand is North East of Australia. No, it is South East of Australia.
- People remember a movie called "Shazaam" that featured a character called "Sinbad" in the 1990's. However, there was no such show.
- Darth Vader in Star Wars said "Luke, I am your Father." Darth Vader actually said "No, I am your father."

It is strange that so many people have false memories, and all believe the same thing. I have included these Mandela Affects because it is an interesting phenomenon and could indeed be a clue that this life is merely a simulation, and these false memories could be glitches, or they could be clues into our true reality from a creator. It could also be that these false memories come from a parallel universe that has somehow became mixed in with our universe. This is possible considering we live in a multiverse with infinite realities playing out within the game. These could be deliberate signs from source giving us a hint at the truth. Those of you that have seen the movie "The Matrix" may wonder if they are computer glitches like the ones that appear in the movie. Either way they point at the truth that what we are experiencing every day is a game. A computer game or if you prefer a computer simulation.

Plato's allegory of the cave

The great philosopher Plato put forward this very intriguing allegory. He described a group of people (prisoners) who have lived their entire lives chained up and facing a blank wall. This is all they have experienced in their lives; they have never seen the real world. There is a fire behind them, and some other people are moving about behind them but in front of the fire. So, these people moving about in front of the fire cast shadows onto the blank wall. The prisoners who are chained up see these shadows on the wall and they believe these shadows are the true reality of their world. They think the shadows are real beings because this is all they have ever seen. They don't know any different.

Plato posits that one prisoner could become free. This prisoner would finally see the fire and realise that the shadows are fake. This prisoner could escape from the cave and discover that there is a whole new world outside. This prisoner would be able to see that the outside world is so much more real than the shadows he had seen previously. In this allegory, the freed prisoner tries to return to where the other prisoners are so that he can free them also. Upon his return, he is blinded because his eyes are not accustomed to sunlight. The chained-up prisoners would see this blindness and believe they will be harmed if they try to leave the cave. So, they choose to continue living chained up watching just shadows.

What is the meaning of Plato's allegory? The most fundamental meaning is we do not know whether the reality we see in our lives is the true reality or not. Could we be like the chained-up prisoners, believing everything we see to be true when really it is an illusion and there may be a greater reality that we are not aware of? What if one person was somehow able to break free and see a higher and truer reality. If someone did this, they would probably try to tell other people in the world about this higher reality. How would we react if someone tried to tell us that this world we see is an illusion and that there is a higher reality? If we did not believe it, we would probably believe this person is crazy. We would be like the chained-up prisoners because we would dismiss this new information and continue to live in the way we have always lived which of course is a complete illusion. The other chained prisoners could not be convinced, and it is the same in our world.

There are a great number of people who would dismiss every word in this book as crazy talk. That is fine because they are simply not ready to know the truth.

You may believe everything in this book and that is great because you now know the truth but it's quite likely that many of your friends and family are not ready yet to know this truth. That is just the way the world is. At some stage every soul will know the truth about this game we are playing, most likely in a future incarnation. But if you believe now, then you are like the man who escaped from the chains in Plato's cave.

I think this is a masterpiece from Plato. I believe that what he is saying through this allegory is quite revelatory. This reality is just a holographic reality created by a computer. There must be a more fundamental reality that exists somewhere, and we should not dismiss this notion. Is there a reality somewhere that is not part of this computer simulation? Is that place the spiritual world or is it something else? We don't really know but we should keep an open mind on the subject or else we are just like the prisoners in that we are closing our minds off from the truth.

Respected scientist Donald Hoffman has been working on determining what reality may be like outside of this simulation. He strongly believes that the only scientific way to know this is by doing the math. That is what he has been doing. Let us call the reality outside of the simulation "base reality." He believes that space and time do not exist in base reality. That is quite amazing. It is hard to imagine a reality without time and I think it's even harder to imagine a reality without space. How can any reality not have space? It is hard for us to wrap our head around that.

Donald also believes that there is no physicality like we have here and no theory of evolution in base reality. This is all supported by the math he has been doing. He believes that base reality could be a kind of conscious network where conscious agents interact with each other not to dissimilar to the way the social media tool twitter works.

Donald is quite a brilliant thinker, and he has several YouTube videos on this subject including an excellent Ted talk entitled "Do we see reality as it is?" Another video he has shot is entitled "Is reality an illusion?" If you are interested in the underlying science which backs up the claims I am making here in this book, then I highly recommend you check out his videos on YouTube. This idea of our reality being a holographic computer simulation is not just limited to the world of spirituality. It is brilliant minds like Donald

Hoffman and other respected physicists who have done the serious math on the subject who say that the evidence is irrefutable- this reality is not real.

Nothing really matters

I would like to finish this chapter with some content about meaning, given that we now know that this life is just a holographic illusion and we as individual humans are holograms too. We are just characters in a computer game. If this is true what does this mean for our lives? Do our lives have any meaning? When you think about it, given these facts it follows that nothing you do in your life really matters. Some people may find this thought a little depressing. You may have spent most of a lifetime chasing success in your career. Or you have dedicated your life for a cause. It doesn't feel good when you find out the entire thing is just a game being played out by a computer simulation.

We must get past this. Life is really about experience and growth. This computer game gives us just that. We must get past feeling depressed that the world is not as real as you thought it was. Life is extraordinary even if it is not real. We get to express ourselves in the most incredible game that has ever been devised. How good is that? We get to experience life richly. We get to grow in terms of personal development and our soul is evolving higher and higher all the time. This is enough. Its more than enough. We are alive and kicking and we are a part of something which is astonishingly and incredibly beautiful. There still is a lot of meaning in our lives and I will go deep into this in Chapter 5 - The Meaning of Life.

Knowing that life is not real can actually help you a lot. For example; some people care a lot about what others think about them. In fact, a lot of people are like that. These people could be people pleasers or maybe show-offs trying to impress others. Maybe these people have a mask or a certain image that they present to the world. You may notice if you are using social media tools like Facebook that some people, by the content of their posts, seem to have perfect lives. Of-course they don't. They are simply picking and choosing what they post online.

It is true that many people care deeply about how they are perceived by others. Would these people care so much if they knew the truth that the others they are trying to impress are just holograms and in fact the whole world is simply a holographic image in a very advanced computer simulation? Would these same people care so much if they knew that this computer game has infinite versions of every event playing out somewhere? You have simply lived out one of these events. This event you lived out is no better or worse than any of the other infinite versions of this same event which exist in the game. It is no more real than any of the other versions. **It's just that you selected this particular version of events through the creation process.** When you consider this, it seems so silly to go through life trying to impress others all the time.

Your soul does not want you to be an actor in the world trying to please or impress everyone you come across. Your soul wants you to be real. Your soul wants you to be your authentic self. You can use the knowledge that this is a computer game to help you be authentic and honest and not an actor. After all, what is the point trying to impress characters in a video game. **The truth about the nature of life can free you from the bondage of people pleasing or trying to impress others.** Accepting the truth really is very liberating. It takes all the worry and stress away.

Another thing is you don't worry so much about mistakes you have made in the past. **Who cares** so much when it's just a computer game where these mistakes were made. Are you getting this? Can you see just how liberating this knowledge is? It frees you. It frees you from emotional suffering. Understanding and believing what I'm writing about here takes you a long way towards becoming spiritually enlightened. I will explain this further in the next chapter.

At your essence, you are not even the person that you seem to be. So, if the person has done a lot of bad things and made a lot of mistakes, **who cares**? Because that person is not the true you at your essence. You are a divine soul (God) remember. The separate person is just an illusion. **You are just playing a game for a short while where you pretend to be a person.** This knowledge frees you from the pressures in life.

I'm not saying "Who cares? Do what you want and ignore any damage you have done" If you break the law, you might go to prison and that will feel very real to you. If you behave badly in life, you will not feel good. You will not be happy, and you will not progress much in your next incarnation either.

I'm saying be the best version of yourself you can be. It's just that if you do make mistakes don't ruminate on them. Let them go because life is just a short computer game. **Those mistakes were made by a hologram with no free will.** Thinking this way gives you incredible freedom.

I said above "**Who cares** when it's just a computer game where these mistakes were made." I want to be very clear here. That is okay at the highest level but it's not okay at the human level. There is a term in spirituality that refers to people who say "I don't care about the hurt I've caused because I don't exist as a separate individual and nothing is real anyway."

This is called **spiritual bypassing** and it's not a good thing to do. Yes that statement is true but on the human level some hurt was experienced and this needs to be acknowledged. So, on the human level one should care for the other person's feelings and make amends. At the highest level some hurt occurred within awareness but It should be addressed at the human level.

One should show sympathy, kindness and try to heal the pain that was experienced within awareness. When one does this then they are not spiritual bypassing. Spiritual bypassing is using the ultimate truth that there is no separate self as an excuse for bad behaviour.

So a combination of the two ways of looking at this type of thing is best. Do what you can to remedy any situation like this at the human level first and then let go of it completely from the true ultimate reality's viewpoint. It is that simple. Let it go and carry on with your life carrying no guilt, no shame, no embarrassment, no regret.

Chapter 4
Become Spiritually Enlightened

The haunted house

In June of 2022 I was lucky enough to be on holiday in Vienna. On one day my wife and I went to the large amusement park there and we went on one of the attractions. It was a ghost train or a haunted house train. We were on a simple cart zig zagging in the dark through a haunted house with all sorts of scary images lighting up or jumping out at us. Was I scared? No, I wasn't. Why? Because I knew it wasn't real. I was simply on a ride. Rather than be scared I was actually entertained. The entire time I was zigzagging past all the scary things I knew that this was not real. I knew it was just an illusion.

This is exactly the same as life. It is the same as the haunted house ride. It is not real. When we go through life holding this realisation in our awareness we cease to suffer. Yes, that is right, we cease to suffer. Life becomes fun. We become happy and blissful. This is the beauty of enlightenment. The key is to remember this life is just a game. We are a soul who is taking a ride just like people on the haunted house ride. So, all you need to do is keep this realisation in your mind. I didn't forget I was on the haunted house ride and freak out mid ride. In the same way you must not forget this life is not real as you go about life. Keep it in mind at all times. By this I mean just keeping it in the background of your mind. It's very easy to do with practice. This is the absolute key piece of information in this book. If you take just one thing out of this book, let it be this.

In this chapter I will present you with eight truth bombs. These are eight laws of reality. I would like you to be so familiar with these laws of reality that you can keep them all easily in the background of your mind as you live life. I have already asked you to keep the truth that life is not real in the back of your mind always. There are seven other truth bombs or laws of reality to come in this chapter. You need to be able to hold the knowledge of all eight truth bombs in the back of your mind at all times. This sounds hard but it's not. Is it hard to remember you are on a haunted house amusement park ride whilst you are riding it? No, it's easy. You do it without thinking. It comes naturally. This is really the key. Everyone who goes on the haunted house ride knows full well the whole time that this is just an amusement park ride. The knowledge doesn't leave them. It is imprinted in their mind. It is completely obvious to them. It is the same for all eight truth bombs. The knowledge that you have of all eight truth bombs should be 100% imprinted in your mind. **You don't forget this knowledge**. It is with you all the time and it too is completely obvious. You will be so familiar with each truth bomb that you will believe each one completely and you will be able to do this easily.

This is all a game. The person you think you are, is not real. It will exist as a hologram for roughly 90 years, that is all. You are God, a divine soul who can never die. You are simply right now playing a holographic computer game which is similar in many ways to the haunted house ride in that it is not real.

This chapter is the most important in this book because it tells you what is required to take most of your suffering in life away. This is the power of being enlightened. **Enlightenment is simply seeing reality as it really is.** Rather than start this chapter with a rather dull definition of what spiritual enlightenment is, I decided to give this very simple analogy. Because to be enlightened, you just need to wake up to the reality that you don't exist as the person you think you are, and that this life is just a computer simulation. You are really a divine soul (God) who can never die. That's it! That is all it takes. You have to wake up to this fact. There is only one "but." What is the "but," that makes all the difference? You have to truly **believe** it!

How do you believe this truth that you don't exist as the individual person you think you are? How do you believe this truth the world is a holographic computer simulation? Easy, you just decide to. That's it, you just make the decision. Will you be perfect making this change right from the start? No, probably not, but stick with it and practice remembering the truth and you will get there.

Firstly, you must believe, but there is a further step which entrenches you in enlightenment. Instead of believing the truth, it is knowing the truth. You start with believing and as time goes on you believe more and more until it gets to the point where you have no doubt at all, and you just know. Here is an example; do you believe the sun will come up tomorrow morning? You know it will. In the same way you can know you are just a hologram, and you can know the universe is also a hologram. If you believe something it implies that you might be wrong, but when you know something then you are much more certain.

The person is not real so the person cannot be enlightened

In the movie franchise Star Wars, Luke Skywalker uses the Jedi mind trick to force other characters to follow his will. It's a great trick and a really fun part of the movies. Luke Skywalker is played by Mark Hamill. Imagine if Mark was hanging out with his co-star Harrison Ford after filming one day and he forgot that Luke Skywalker was not real. He decides to use the Jedi mind trick on Harrison and says, "Harrison, you will bring me a cold beer right now." It could be a funny joke, right? But what if Mark was serious? What if he forgot that he wasn't really Luke Skywalker? Sounds pretty ridiculous, doesn't it? Yet this is what the vast majority of us are doing.

Because of the veil of illusion, we are forgetting that we are a divine soul and that this person we think we are is not real. Remembering that this person we think we are is not real is the key part of becoming spiritually enlightened. If you think you are this person you seem to be, then you cannot become enlightened.

In truth you are already enlightened, it's just that this person or character you are playing is getting in the way and stopping you from realising the truth. In a way you could say that everyone on Earth is already enlightened. That is roughly 8 billion people. What these people need to do is to realise or make real what being enlightened is. To actualise it. To do that they need to drop believing they are a person. How do you do that? You just decide. You decide to drop this belief and you decide to believe everything that is written in this book. Everything you need to know to become enlightened is written in this book. **You don't need religion and you don't need to travel the world trying to find yourself.** Somehow you have found your way to this book and that didn't happen by accident. Everything happens for a reason. It could be that you think this is all nonsense and maybe this book has found you just so that a seed of truth can be implanted in your mind. Maybe this book has found you because you are ready now after many incarnations to understand why you are alive and what is going on here.

What are the benefits of spiritual enlightenment?

The first benefit is that you will cease to have so much emotional suffering. As individuals we are built to suffer. This is because of our ego. We worry. We feel regret. We get anxious. This is all on a good day. On a bad day we hate ourselves. We hate our enemies. We feel depressed about our life. The ego is just built to suffer. It is the nature of being a separate individual person. When you realise a truth like the fact you are everyone on the planet, you don't need to feel guilty that the dream character you seem to be had too much for lunch for example or was angry with their partner. It just doesn't seem important anymore. That is the kind of relief from suffering you get when you remember you are not an individual person but one with everyone in this computer simulation.

One of the reasons we suffer so much is that this game we are playing on Earth is a very difficult one. It is one of the toughest planets to incarnate on. We come here to learn lessons. We generally learn our lessons by one of two ways. Firstly, by having an insight into something. This could be a minor insight or all the way up to an epiphany. The second way we learn our lessons is through pain and suffering. Sometimes we need to suffer for a very long time before we finally learn the lesson which is at the bottom of all the suffering. Another way to look at this is to see suffering as our teacher. We can even express this in another way. We could say...

If someone is not enlightened, it just means they have not suffered enough.

All this suffering we experience is happening so that we get to the point where we say "Enough, I let go of believing I exist as an individual. I will look at life in a different way now. I will see it as it really is."

The more suffering you have had in your life the easier it is for you to wake up and become enlightened. There is more chance of a drug addicted criminal in prison waking up than a celebrity multi-millionaire. I can safely say this just on the basis that the drug addict has most likely had more suffering in their life. **This is because those people who suffer look inwards to find meaning.** Life has been so hard on them, and they are in so much pain that they cry out for liberation, and they look within to find out why life is so hard and what the point of living is.

It's all set up in this way. **We are meant to suffer so that we look within to find meaning, and this is the way we eventually can transcend the ego (the belief we are a separate individual person) and become spiritually enlightened.** Looking within is the first step. Once we start looking within, we always find a lot more than we bargained for. A lot more. Looking within is usually followed by a period of time seeking. Seeking is a term for those people on the spiritual path trying to find answers to the big existential questions. Hopefully following this path (usually after a number of years seeking) leads you to uncover the treasure which is spiritual enlightenment. **Enlightenment when you attain it is the end of seeking** and it is also the end of suffering. **So, there is a prize at the end for those that suffer.** Those people who have an easy life may not suffer so much but they also have less chance of becoming enlightened.

This is why Earth is considered to be so tough. It is not for the faint hearted. It takes real courage to incarnate and live a life here. Until we go all the way to spiritual enlightenment we will continue to suffer in life. Some people will suffer more than others, but we all will experience suffering. It does not matter how much personal development you do. Personal development will help but it will not stop all suffering. The only way out is through spiritual enlightenment.

Many people say "Why does a loving God allow so much suffering to happen in the world?" The answer is because we as souls chose to have this suffering to wake ourselves up and eventually get the prize that is enlightenment. **Suffering is our teacher**. Without suffering we would just get by day to day, lifetime after lifetime without ever knowing the truth. Life would be easy, but we would not learn anything and we would not evolve. Source knows that we as souls are completely safe here playing this game. No soul can ever be injured in the game. The human body can be injured but the soul is indestructible. Source is like a loving parent happily knowing their child is safe playing in the backyard.

You may be thinking; "I don't think I suffer that much." It is true that some people only suffer lightly compared to others. You may be this way. I want to tell you something. Don't wait until you suffer. Wake up now anyway. You don't have to wait for a life crisis to become enlightened you can do it at any time. So do it now and you will avoid the unnecessary suffering that will eventually get you. Either in this lifetime or the next.

Transcending suffering is the first benefit of enlightenment, and the second benefit is that you will experience bliss, peace as well as pure happiness. Happiness, believe it or not, is our natural state and when we strip away all the ego, this is what we are left with. People often say things like "I just want to be happy." They believe they must add something to themselves to achieve this. They think they will be happy if they have a new car or renovate their kitchen. Maybe if they changed jobs or emigrated to a different country they will be happy. In fact, it's the opposite. They don't need to add anything to their life. They need to take away the ego or the individual self to reveal what was there all along. A natural state of happiness. A happiness which had just been covered up.

A newborn baby, a day old will experience this pure bliss. This is because they have not yet formed an ego. They have not been conditioned by society. All babies bask in the natural state of happiness. Unfortunately, as they grow up the conditioning of society affects them, and they form an ego. They start acting out a dream character (the individual person). This natural state of happiness gets covered up by layers of conditioning. It's only by reversing this process that we can return to living in bliss.

Giving up the personal self is harder for some

You are already enlightened but unfortunately you are not experiencing the benefits of it. You are already enlightened because you are already God. That is a done deal. You are already it. There is just something that is in the way, stopping you enjoying the benefits of being the supreme creator. It's that little individual self you still think you are. The dream character or the ego.

It is because you still believe you are the dream character or the lead actor in the movie just like Mark Hamill believing he is still Luke Skywalker. I have hinted at this already that if you have been relatively successful (success can be measured by many ways) in your life, then it is probably going to be harder for you to let go of being the dream character or ego you think you are. The reasons are obvious. You have done well in life. You appear at least to have everything going for you and of course it's hard to let go of that.

Conversely, if your life has not been successful (by traditional measures of success) then you will probably find it easier to let go of the dream character. If you have failed at everything you have ever tried to do, then it is relatively easier for you. What all this means is that if your life has been tough and you find yourself really down on your luck, then you have an easier path than someone who seems to just keep winning in this computer game of life.

What does transcending the personal self mean? Do I have to die?

No, you don't have to physically die. You will still have to live as an individual human. That's just the way this computer game works. It's just that deep down you need to know life is just an illusion. You continue to act as an individual self, but you keep the truth in your awareness that you are a divine soul. You just play along with the game. It's that simple. All you need to do is to just hold the knowledge of what is real as you go about life as a seeming individual human being.

Putting this into practice

In this next section of the book, I will ask you to hold some knowledge in your awareness that we learnt earlier in Chapter 1. Sometimes it helps to think it through step by step especially as we are just beginning to see reality as it really is. So, feel free to do this. Eventually you will get to the point where this knowledge is second nature to you. You will just have a knowing of it which you hold in your awareness. Holding knowledge in your awareness is really the key to changing your life.

Most people who read this book will not follow through and apply this knowledge in their life. Those that do decide to live their lives based on the truths in this book will find life becomes infinitely easier. You will overcome most of your emotional suffering. If you suspect you might soon forget what is written here and that you will return to your default way of playing this game, then I suggest not filing this book away in your bookshelf. Keep it out on your bedroom chest of drawers or your coffee table. Open it up randomly every day and read a few passages. This will help you to live the truths spoken of here.

Transcending ego or transcending the person

Hopefully now it's clear that you need to see through the illusion that you are just a person. We have learnt already that your ego is a collection of thoughts about this person who you seem to be. Transcending the ego or transcending the person is basically the same thing. To transcend ego, what we need to do is to remember the truth and then align with this truth. This means ceasing to see ourselves as an ego or person. This is a radical shift.

Let's re-cap some of what we have learnt. Here are three truth bombs:

Truth Bomb 1:
We are a divine soul made of divine consciousness.
Truth Bomb 2:
We are the entire universe and everything in the universe is one.
Truth Bomb 3:
We create our own reality, and everything happens for a good reason.

I would like to present two examples of a situation involving a person and explain how we can deal with these situations and transcend believing we are the person. We will need to keep these truth bombs above in our awareness. This is why I'd like you to become very familiar with this knowledge. So, it becomes so familiar it's locked into your subconscious mind.

I am not trying to tell you how you should act if you were in a situation like this. You are obviously free to act and say whatever you wish. I am simply giving two random examples and am illustrating how you could see these situations from the level of the soul. The key point, I'm trying to make is just the shift up to big picture reality. There is never a script that you should follow in your interactions with people. My advice for all interactions is that you are always authentic and real.

In the first example someone is being praised and in the second a person is being criticised. I have chosen these two scenarios as the ego is very sensitive to praise and criticism. The ego naturally responds to praise with pride and to criticism with guilt.

Example 1: Feedback from your boss at work *"Congratulations Elaine on that deal you worked on last week. That was outstanding work."*

Let's now analyse what has happened here using the three truth bombs from above.

1. ***We are a divine soul made of divine consciousness***: I am not really this individual self or ego called Elaine. I am more than just this. Elaine is an illusion so that life can work properly. I need to look at this comment

from a bigger perspective. I must not fall into the trap of thinking I am just this one person, Elaine. It is tempting to do that because Elaine is being praised in this situation. I will look at the big picture reality instead. I am really a divine soul made of consciousness and my boss is too. What is really happening here? A divine soul is speaking to a divine soul or in more general terms God is speaking to God.

2. ***We are the entire universe and everything in the universe is one***: I am the entire workplace and all the staff employed by the workplace so I should see this praise from the point of view of the whole work team. There is no separation between anyone in the team at work. They are all one. I can see that the workplace is functioning well. Communication is open and transparent. I am grateful to have this job and my boss. I see this comment as a sign of good strong leadership from my boss just as much as what it says about Elaine.

3. ***I create my own reality, and everything happens for a good reason***: I have manifested this situation so I need to understand why this may be happening and what I could learn from it. Maybe it was to remind myself that a happy well-functioning team at work is important and that I seem to be on the right track with my career right now

Can you see how we are seeing this situation through the prism of big picture reality? This is all we need to do.

   Example 2: Feedback from your next-door neighbour *"Harry, why the hell did you not take more care with putting your trash out? Honestly, there are pieces of trash blowing in the wind halfway down the street"*

   Once again, we remind ourselves:

1. ***We are a divine soul made of divine consciousness***: I am not really this individual self or ego called Harry. I am more than this. Harry is an illusion so that life can work properly. I need to look at this criticism from a bigger perspective. I must let this criticism go without an emotional reaction. I must not get angry. I do not respond by defending my position or casting blame on someone else. I also do not allow my ego to make me feel guilty. The seeming individual self is not perfect

and things like this will occur, so I am okay with this criticism. What is really happening here? A divine soul is speaking to a divine soul or more generally God is speaking to God.

2. ***We are the entire universe and everything in the universe is one***: I am one with my neighbour so I must consider this situation from his point of view. I can understand that this has affected him. From his point of view, it would be frustrating seeing trash on the ground. I am also one with all the neighbours on the street so I will consider how this has affected them too.

3. ***I create my own reality, and everything happens for a good reason***: I have manifested this situation so I need to understand why this may be happening and what could I learn from it. Maybe it happened so that I could improve my empathy towards all my neighbours, and it also reminds me I am living in a very good community of people. In the grand scheme of things this is not a big deal, and I can apologise to my next-door neighbour and move on.

Can you see how we are viewing this situation through the prism of big picture reality instead of through the prism of an individual self?

I never said this would be easy, but this is what is needed to transcend ego. It requires a kind of symbolic death of the ego. Spiritual teachers sometime describe this process as **learning to die before you die**. I like this phrase as it evokes the enormity of the change in perspective required. We are ceasing to see ourselves as a person. This is a shift from illusion to reality. These are obviously just two examples. In life, you are going to get many examples of praise and criticism and lots of other completely different scenarios as well. Everyday there are many situations where you could apply these truth bombs. In fact, this truth can be applied to every possible scenario you could ever find yourself. No matter what the situation is you can choose to see that situation through realities prism.

What you need to do now is **become an expert at seeing events in your life through the lens of reality** just like I have done above. Interacting with the world while holding truth bombs in your awareness is how you enlighten yourself.

It is quite easy to do. You don't need to recreate word for word what I have done above. You just need to understand the process and have the same general idea that I have applied above. So, it will be different every time you do it but if you keep this general idea of reality in mind, you will be fine.

Reality or illusion - you choose

Do you want to live in reality or illusion? That is the choice here. Just because 99.999997% of people are living in illusion, does that mean you should too? Because living in the egoic state is not reality. It is far from reality. It is an altered state. If you want to live in an altered state, then stick with living though your ego. You don't need to take any drugs to alter reality as ego is already doing that for you. On the other hand, if you want to be one of the very few people who know what reality really is and have enough courage to live it, then you can literally change your life. You can cease to suffer. Here is the summary of the three truth bombs again:

Truth Bomb 1:
We are a divine soul made of divine consciousness.
Truth Bomb 2:
We are the entire universe and everything in the universe is one.
Truth Bomb 3:
We create our own reality, and everything happens for a good reason.

There are of course, many more truths to reality than just these, but these three pieces of truth will take you a long way. It just takes practice. You must automatically go back to the truth above. You have heard the expression "she lost the plot." The plot is not what you have been taught. I would love you to "keep the plot." Keeping the plot is akin to understanding the truths above. You need to carry this knowledge around with you 24/7 and apply it in every situation.

The key is to apply it, to live it. The reason I am emphasising the importance of living out this truth is because these truths are basic tenets of spirituality. Many spiritual people know and understand this basic knowledge. But as soon as something goes wrong in their life, they forget this entirely and react as a person. They don't realise how incredibly powerful these truths are if you just apply it and live it. I would say 99% of these spiritual seekers automatically fall back into being a person if they are praised or criticised.

Why practice, practice, practice can lead you to enlightenment.

Some people spend 20, 30 or even 40 years seeking enlightenment. Often to no avail. The problem with seeking or searching is that you identify as a seeker. If you are identified as a seeker, then you cannot at the same time identify correctly as God. There are people who travel to India looking for a guru to follow and attend meditations and retreats all over the world and despite all this they are not enlightened. The reason is because they are very identified with being this spiritual seeker. As long as you are a seeker you can never actually arrive. Your life will all become seeking.

For these people the experience of peace and happiness from enlightenment is deemed missing, so that is why they go out seeking and searching all over the world to find enlightenment. The funny thing is, that what they were searching for, they already had. They were already enlightened and happiness was their birthright. The problem though was that the ego was in the way of realising that happiness.

It is important to understand that to become enlightened you must start seeing reality as it is, right now in the present moment. You have to start right now. Not in six months' time. Not after you have attended some spiritual workshops or travelled to Nepal. However, the strategies I am giving you in this chapter can and should be practiced by you. There is a paradox here. You can only achieve enlightenment in the present moment but practicing seeing reality as it is, brings you closer to enlightenment.

There is a reason practice helps. I have already explained that the key is belief. You must believe the truths being outlined here. Sometimes when we practice, we start to believe a little more. We become more familiar with it all. What seems way out and strange at the start begins to feel more believable. We become used to the concepts and consciously and unconsciously we really start to believe. When we truly believe, that is when the magic happens. The ultimate is when we go even further than believing and **know** deep down that the truth bombs are all accurate.

For most people becoming enlightened is not an instant event followed by lifelong bliss. It was however for spiritual teacher Eckhart Tolle. When Eckhart experienced enlightenment for the first time it was so complete, he spent the next two years sitting on a park bench in total bliss. He has now gone on to be one of the most respected spiritual teachers in the world. He still feels bliss from time to time and he has a rock-solid feeling of absolute peace that never goes away.

This type of enlightenment is sometimes called Sudden Awakening (also known as Sudden Realisation or Sudden Illumination). In Zen Buddhism, the classical term is (Du'nwu'). This contrasts with (Jia'nwu') the term for the more common Gradual Awakening or Gradual Enlightenment. In the case of a sudden awakening what usually happens is that we all of a sudden have an instant epiphany. This is a moment in time, an enlightenment experience where it just all suddenly clicks, we let go of being a person (ego) and see reality as it really is. We feel instantly blissful and uplifted. At this early stage of enlightenment the bliss is usually very strong and it can stay with you for a long time. You could have constant bliss for months or even a few years. After this initial period what happens is that the bliss will start to come and go. It will stay like this for the rest of your life. What is constant however is peace. Even if you are not feeling blissful at a certain point in time you will be feeling a beautiful feeling of peace. This is the true meaning of the peace of Christ. You feel peaceful because you know that there is absolutely nothing in the game to worry about. You know the game is not real and you know it's always perfect. So why worry?

To maintain the amazing bliss and peace of spiritual enlightenment you must be aligned with reality. You must continue to see reality as it really is even after you have achieved enlightenment. If you cease to do this and slip back into ego, then the bliss and peace will go and suffering will return.

Alignment has nothing to do with outcomes. Even if a so-called bad outcome occurs, you can still be in alignment by not blaming yourself or others. Realise that it was simply fate, be positive and move on. Alignment can be measured by which emotions we are feeling. Emotions are a barometer for alignment. If you are feeling good, you know you are most likely in alignment with reality. If you are feeling some negative emotions, you must ask yourself where is it that I am not aligned with truth. Then ask yourself how you can change the way you are thinking to align with truth. In this way you can use your emotions to judge how aligned you are.

The key thing is to keep practicing holding reality in your awareness. The more you practice the more you start to believe.

More truth bombs

I would like to present some more truth bombs for you to hold in your awareness or to think through as you go about playing this game. Just like the three we have already covered, staying aware of these truths will help you transcend believing you are a person. What you need to do is apply the same way of thinking we used with the three truth bombs previously.

Break down your interactions with people and the world in the same way except this time with this different truth bomb. See the situation you are in through the prism of this truth bomb. Do the same for the truth bombs which follow too. These truth bombs can be applied to any situation you find yourself in.

Truth Bomb 4:
Everything we see around us is an illusion. Everything, including our bodies is a holographic projection.

Again, it's a case of holding this truth bomb in our awareness. Practice, practice, practice. The more you practice the more you believe. When you really truly believe that is when enlightenment can hit you. You are a hologram, it's as simple as that. If you are arguing with or have been hurt by someone else, know that they are a hologram too. Everything in the entire multiverse is a hologram.

This is a computer game we are playing and it's a holographic kind of game. Nothing at all is real except for the actual consciousness we experience playing this game. Consciousness is another word for God. So, you could say that all that there is here, is God.

Every single situation or place you could ever find yourself in, is simply holographic in nature. It's all part of the game you are playing and its always 100% perfect. This means that no matter what is happening to you, it's exactly what should be happening to you. So, couple this idea with the former and you have:

Everything around me is a holographic illusion and its exactly perfect for my souls wishes.

So, no matter how bad the situation may seem it's what your soul wants. This realisation alone can bring you peace instead of frustration or anger.

Just accept what is happening to you and rest assured its exactly what your soul wants. What a relief to realise that nothing has gone wrong. You have not messed up. It's meant to be this way. You may not realise why it's meant to be this way, but it doesn't matter because whatever is happening to you is always perfect otherwise it would not be happening.

Can you see how holding this truth bomb in your awareness or thinking this through can deliver you great rewards. It can also bring you spiritual enlightenment. If you believe it enough, it can be a trigger for an enlightenment experience. A breakthrough where you suddenly see life as it really is.

Truth Bomb 5:
You are that other person, and they are you.

This truth bomb is really powerful. Keep this in mind when you are chatting to your work colleague or when spending time with your family. It's especially powerful if you are with someone you dislike. You dislike them but then you remember you are them and they are you. This is not just a trick of the mind, its 100% true. Holding this truth in your awareness can act as an antidote to negative emotions like dislike, distrust or even envy. When we remember we are our enemy it dissolves powerful negative emotions like hate. It is harder to hate someone when you know you are that person.

Let's re-cap why this is true. Source divided himself up into souls to go out and play this computer game. Your enemy is just one of these souls just like you. You both come from source, so you are both God. There is only one God and that is why you are both one. Eventually both your soul and the soul of your enemy will return to source and reunite.

This truth bomb can be practiced in every single situation in the game when you are interacting with another person. So, there are many, many opportunities to practice.

When we walk past that homeless person on the street. They are us. When we see that celebrity on TV or online. We are them. We are the best of us, and we are the worst of us. We are heads of state and leaders of nations, and we are also criminals in prison. When we use this truth bomb it completely transforms how we see people. In the past we used to compare ourselves with others. We would think things like, "I am doing better than that homeless person." Or we would think "why is she a celebrity and I am not? I am just as talented as her." We can no longer think this because these truth bombs are to be taken literally. We really are that homeless person. We already are that celebrity. The world leader truly is us. This new way of seeing the world is transformative.

Truth Bomb 6:
Every person I see is really God

Practice seeing past the illusion. Know in your heart that every person you cast your eyes upon is really God (whether they know it or not). Whether you are speaking to a child or a 100-year-old man, remember the truth. When we remember this, then we honour the divine soul we are interacting with, and it can be enough to give us a taste of enlightenment. Again, the key element is belief. We need to see past the personality, see past your history with the person, see past their appearance. God can have any personality and any appearance. With practice we get more familiar with this truth bomb and with practice we start to believe more and more.

It is not just other people who are God. You are God too. I am being as literal as possible. You are literally God.

I want to now talk about knowing you are God when you are in some kind of conflict with someone else. It can be hard when you are in the heat of the moment to say to yourself "you know what, I'm not this person I seem to be, I am actually God." Especially if you are experiencing some kind of emotional suffering and feeling emotions like anger or frustration. However, it is difficult situations like these where we really need to know we are God. If you are in a situation like this, ask yourself "do I want to hang on to personhood (believing I'm a person) in this moment?" If you are too angry to let go of personhood, then you will obviously continue to suffer. It takes a lot of courage to rise above your anger and frustration and let go of personhood and instead see yourself as God interacting with God.

When we are angry, we are very heavily identifying with ego and that is why it is so hard to let go of personhood. The first time you do this will require a mammoth effort however the reward is life changing. If you can do this, you are choosing to rise above the drama in your life and that is a pretty incredible thing to do. If you can let go of personhood in the middle of some kind of drama and know yourself as God, then you are displaying a very advanced state of consciousness. Very few people can do this. Your reward for doing so is transcending emotional suffering.

It is not just in the heat of the moment when it helps to remember who you are. It helps to do this when our minds take us back into the past through memories. How often do you mull over past events feeling emotions like regret? This is also a time to let go of personhood. Remind yourself that you are not this person you seem to be and that you are in fact the creator of the game.

This truth bomb can be used in many situations to cut through. It is very versatile. In fact, it is possible to realise spiritual enlightenment by just using this one truth bomb alone. The truth be told is that the same applies to all the other truth bombs too. However, a knowledge of all the truth bombs prepares you the best to see reality as it really is.

Seeing into why something is happening can bring an enlightenment experience.

Just being able to see why something is unfolding can tip you into an experience of enlightenment. As you grow and gain in wisdom it is not hard to see why something may be happening. For example, it could be karma at play as to why you experience some kind of loss. Just being able to see this and be okay with it can bring you an enlightenment experience. The key is to be able to get an insight into why some thing is happening. Is there a lesson in this situation? Is the universe trying to send you a message? If the answer is yes then what is the message? Is this happening so that you will experience growth? Whenever we think like this, we are aligning with reality, and this is why sometimes just having an insight can give you a taste of enlightenment.

Practice trying to see why things are happening. Do the best you can. Don't expect miracles straight away. Just keep at it. You may experience enlightenment straight away, but for most people it will take time. Remember the paradox that you can only be enlightened in the present moment, but practice can help you attain enlightenment in the future.

Gossip

We have all done it at some stage in our life. I am talking about taking pleasure at someone else's misfortune. Another thing we do is gossip and many of us do this too. All this activity is ego based. We gossip about someone else because we believe they are a separate individual from us. It is clearly based on a delusion (that we are all separate).

The reality is that we are all one. So clearly if we delight in someone else's misfortune or gossip about them, we are aligning ourselves with a lie. We are living very much in ego. It is incredibly powerful to see through this delusion and resist gossip. When we refuse to gossip, we are aligning ourselves with reality. We know we are that other person, and we know that the other person is us. We are seeing reality as it really is and just doing this can be enough to trigger an enlightenment experience.

Another thing we can avoid is reading or opening stories on the internet that are gossip type stories. We can rise above this need to read about others failings. It can seem innocuous to read a story on your phone about someone else being in a tough spot but every time we do this, we are announcing to the universe that we believe we are an ego. We are announcing that we are deluded and believe this big illusion. When we don't do it, we are announcing the opposite. We are declaring that we know the truth. We are all one and we are all God.

If you want to become enlightened, you really need to take this onboard. You must stop judging other people. **They are you and you are them**. If you believe this, then there is no need to judge others because the reality is you are judging yourself. Be kind to people. Treat them as you would like to be treated. Remind yourself when you are interacting with people that you are one with them and that one thing is God. Let's say you are having a one-on-one phone conversation with a work colleague. Ask yourself- what is really happening here? The answer is that **God is talking to God**. You must start seeing life in this way because this is reality. This is truth. When you choose not to gossip you are aligning yourself with reality. You are aligning yourself with what is true.

How many times have you read articles on your phone or in a publication about an individual who has made the news for all the wrong reasons? How many times have you seen on television a news story about someone falling foul of the law? That's you they are talking about. You are the one who has made news. Become aware of this. See it in this light. The reverse is also true. Let's say you watch a sports news report on television about an athlete breaking a world record. Once again that person is you. **You must start seeing life through this prism of oneness.** This is a fundamental change in how you view the world.

Ego will try to trick you

Be aware of any negative thoughts that you might be getting when you practice seeing reality as it really is. You might have thoughts like; "This is silly,'" or "I am no good at this."

Ignore thoughts like these. The ego will give you thoughts like this and this is because the ego feels threatened. The ego knows its days are numbered. It will fight desperately to stay alive and keep you believing in it. It will bombard you with negative thoughts, so just let them pass and try not to attach onto these thoughts.

The ego will even try to keep the identity of the spiritual seeker going. The ego likes being the spiritual seeker. The reason is because as long as you are seeking then you are not finding, so it is still safe. The ego likes being spiritual. This is called the spiritual ego and it is a trap many people fall into. Some people feel superior just because they are spiritual. This of course is all ego activity (I am spiritual, and you are not so therefore I am better than you). This is very common. The irony is that the very people who want enlightenment, push it away because they get an ego boost out of being a spiritual person.

Remember that the ego is a product of natural selection and evolution. It has helped humans stay alive for thousands of years. It is just a collection of beliefs that describe the seeming individual self. It is a computer program. But it is no longer necessary. We have evolved to the point where we don't need the ego anymore. We have arrived at the point of our evolution where we are ready to upgrade our ego computer program to a God computer program. Expect one hell of a fight from the ego. It will not lie down and just die. It will throw everything it can at you to stay relevant.

Ego mind attacks

The spiritual master Mooji describes the phenomenon of the ego trying desperately to keep control as "mind attacks." I love this description as it hints at just how hard the ego will come at you once you stop seeing the game through its distorted prism. The ego will not go down without a fight.

The term "mind attack" conjures up a feeling of a war being played out. This is not wrong. It can feel like a war. It can feel like a series of battles. In each battle the ego is desperate for you to identify with it. Remember the ego is a collection of beliefs about the individual or separate person. The ego does not care whether these beliefs are negative or positive as long as you are identifying with the person. So, expect the ego to throw a life crisis at you.

I hate to see people going through hell, but this is the reality of what the ego will do to try and keep control. It will quite likely throw a once in a lifetime crisis at you. It will take all your powers to rise above it and not see the reality being played out through the prism of the individual self. The ego will deliberately target your weak links. It is fighting for survival so it will look to exploit any weakness you have. This is what a "mind attack" is. You will need to get through these battles because it could happen a few times before you finally win the war. Be prepared for your deepest, darkest demons to come out. The ego hasn't needed to use these demons on you before but now that you want to transcend ego it will throw everything it can at you so that it can survive and keep control.

I once went through an event I would describe as a mind attack. A few things all seemed to go wrong at the same time and that lured me into thinking about myself as an ego or an individual person who was having a run of bad things happening to me. I was thinking "poor me." Which of course is thinking about oneself as an ego or individual person. Luckily, I was able to get myself out of this illusion by thinking through a number of truth bombs which pulled me out of the mind attack.

This is what happened; I was flying to another city in New Zealand, where my parents live. I wanted to visit them and I also wanted to attend an event with them that I had been looking forward to for a long time. Shortly after arriving I was starting to feel unwell. I tested myself for Covid and it was negative, so I thought I just had a cold. The day after arriving, myself and my parents headed out to the event. We had only just arrived when the event was called off because of unforeseen circumstances. This was very disappointing, and we had to go back home. I was feeling even more ill by this stage, so I tested myself again and this time I tested positive to Covid. The whole trip seemed to be going wrong.

What happened next was the final straw. I had an argument with my dad. He had said something which triggered me, and I reacted as an ego by defending my position and shooting back accusations at him. I was experiencing a lot of negative thoughts and I was feeling upset. As mentioned earlier everything seemed to be going wrong. I was heavily identifying as an individual ego who had been a victim of a few "bad" things happening to it. I fumed for a short period of time before I realised that I had slipped into ego and that I needed to pull myself out of it and get back to identifying as divine consciousness. At this point I was self-isolating in my room, so I used that opportunity to pull myself out of ego just by thinking through and reminding myself of a number of truth bombs. I will share each of these truth bombs below...

Truth Bomb 7:
Life is not real.

I simply reminded myself of the truth that everything is just a holographic game. It all only takes a few moments in the spirit world. Why was I getting so uptight about what is happening in a computer game? Then it just hit me. **This isn't real.** What was happening with my dad was not real. I am dreaming it. The thing is life feels so real but it's not. I had temporarily forgotten that life is not real. I had been taken in by the illusion. Once I remembered this my anger started to disappear and I felt relief. This is perhaps the broadest of all the truth bombs. It is very simple and kind of sums up everything in the book. It certainly helped me in my argument with my dad. It is just four words (life is not real) but if you are able to believe or even better, know these four words are true then you will find liberation from emotional suffering and attain happiness.

   This truth bomb is particularly powerful if you are like most people and you care what others think about you. You imagine that right now others are thinking bad things about you. You think they are talking to each other saying bad things about you. I have good news for you. They aren't thinking or talking about you because this life is not real. It is just a holographic computer game being played by God. You must understand that the world literally does not exist like you think it does. The game has infinite versions of every situation playing out at the same time and none of this is real. Why worry about one tiny splinter of the multiverse where you feel upset about something. Can you understand that life is not real? The world does not exist. It is all in your mind. If you can grasp and fathom this extraordinary truth, then you will stop thinking there are people behind closed doors thinking and saying bad things about you.

Truth Bomb 8:
I have no free will, life simply unfolds by itself.

The next truth bomb I used to diffuse my argument with my dad was the truth that there is no "do-er with free will." There is no dad doing stuff and there is no me doing stuff. Life simply unfolds by itself. **Free will does not exist like we think it does**. There was no way I could have avoided this situation. Everything is part of a divine plan. This situation was meant to be so why was I resisting it? This is also the idea that everything happens for a good reason. This truth bomb tells us that whatever situation you are in, no matter how bad it is, it is perfection playing out. It was meant to be and perhaps there is a lesson to be learned from this seeming nasty situation.

Truth Bomb 5:
I am Dad and Dad is me and paradoxically neither of us exist.

It was also calming to remember that we are both one. Knowing I am dad, and he is me reversed the negative feelings I was feeling about him. Straight away I had more empathy for my dad in this situation. Instead of seeing my dad as separate from me and defending my position against him, I suddenly felt relief as I remembered I am him. **I realised I had been arguing with myself.**

The second part of this truth bomb is that even though we are each other and we are one, paradoxically we don't actually exist. We just seem to. I was able to use this knowledge to come out of the mind attack I was experiencing with my dad completely. I became fully aware that if the world is not real then that means myself and my dad are not real either. It is normal and natural to resist the notion that you are not real. We want to believe of course that we exist. However, the truth is that we as a human being do not exist. Our existence as a human being is an illusion. **We are really God playing a computer game where the main character is you, the human being, and that is all you are - a character in a computer game**. Can you truly believe that you don't exist? It is possible to play this game by going about life while you hold the knowledge in your mind that you don't exist. In fact, this is the best way to play this game.

The ego mind will automatically resist this idea. It will say, of course, I exist. Here I am right now. I am flesh and blood. It goes against every instinct you have. It belies what you see with your own eyes and what you experience with your senses. That is why it is only souls with a very high level of spiritual evolution who can live this truth. We cannot really understand how this can be so. Don't try to understand it because it is hard to fathom. If you can take this leap of faith and realise that you are just a character in a holographic computer game, you will be astounded at how much easier the game becomes. This is a way you can experience heaven on Earth.

These three truth bombs worked very quickly to calm me down. Then what I did was to deliberately go into the "I am" state by practising presence or mindfulness. I became present by putting my attention inside of my body by noticing my heart. I found the stillness that is "I am." I did my very best to ignore negative thoughts from the mind about my dad or about the situation. **I let the negative thoughts pass without putting my attention on them.** I was aware that my essence was not my thoughts. In this way I didn't identify with my thoughts. I critically appraised my thoughts. I asked myself "are these thoughts really accurate?" So, I refused to identify with my thoughts, and I examined them to see whether they were true or not. I found that they were actually false. The ego was giving me thoughts to inflame the situation, but I did not take the bait.

This is the type of control over the mind you need to have. Stepping back and questioning whether your thoughts are true. You must realise that you are not your thoughts. **You are consciousness which is simply listening in to your thoughts.** You can reject your thoughts as nonsense if you want to.

Anyone who has a spiritual awakening will most likely have to deal with mind attacks. Another thing that happens to people going through a spiritual awakening is something called "dark night of the soul." This is a phase or period of time which is very painful. People going through this feel many negative emotions. They feel lost and can't find any meaning in life anymore. This often comes a year or two after the spiritual awakening begins.

When someone first wakes up and follows the spiritual path, they often find themselves joyful and uplifted but this phase will eventually end. Dark night of the soul comes later in the awakening process. It comes near the end, kind of like a final hurdle to overcome. It is unfortunately going to last more than one night though. It could go on for months or even years. This is not an easy time. It is really hard, but you must just hang in there and do your best not to identify as an ego.

The experience of dark night of the soul often coincides with a loss of meaning. The way in which we have viewed the world has gone and we don't have anything to replace it with. What happens then is we kind of sink. We are forced to face ourselves and face the world with our old model of the world destroyed. This can lead to clinical depression. We can't make sense of anything anymore. An example of this could be someone who has religiously followed the Catholic faith their whole life and when they decide to abandon this faith, they find themselves lost and without meaning.

Dark night of the soul can be very confusing and very hard to cope with, but it is just a stage, and you can get through it and out the other side. The key is to find a new and better world view. This can take some time. Unfortunately, many people turn to self-medication when they are experiencing dark night of the soul. They find that they can cope better using drugs and alcohol. Addiction can be part of the awakening process. I have heard spiritual seekers say things like "my spiritual awakening needs this alcohol right now." It is tempting to use drugs or alcohol if you are experiencing a mind attack or dark night of the soul. This may seem to help at the time, but it is not the answer long term. The real key is to find a new way to view the world. To find meaning in life again.

Seeing reality as it really is

This is not rocket science. You can do this. See how I was able to use the truth bombs to see the situation with my dad in a different way? The truth bombs allowed me to see the situation from reality's point of view not from ego's point of view. I want to now write about how to view every-day life situations because these are the situations you are in all the time and it's how you perceive these everyday situations that is the key to really getting you over the line to an enlightenment experience. The next sentence in this book is very important...

Seeing reality requires you to see every-day life from a different perspective.

Let's have an example of a situation that happens all the time; that is one person chatting to another person. I mentioned this earlier, however it is so important so let's continue to explore this. The normal perspective is that one human being is chatting to a completely separate human being. You won't see it this way however because you will look at this situation through the lens of reality. What is really happening? God is talking to God. You will see this because that is the reality of it. If you are chatting to someone and see their divinity. Keep in mind you are talking to God. This is something that can be learned. As I mentioned earlier in the book it doesn't matter whether you are interacting with a child or an old man, they are God and so of course are you.

Another example may be a football (soccer) match taking place between the national sides of England and Brazil. The normal perspective is that two totally different countries and two power houses of the game are competing against each other for the pride of their respective countries. However, you will not live or die by the result even if you come from one of these countries because you know it is just God competing with God. Can you put aside your patriotism and see reality, or will you be partisan wanting bragging rights after a victory? This doesn't mean you can't enjoy sport. Sure, watch sport and enjoy the skill on display and you can certainly hope your country or team wins. It's just that you will know deep down the truth is that both teams are really one and that one thing is God. So, in reality there is no loser. In this way you can enjoy the illusion and get into the game, but **you don't get totally seduced by the illusion you keep what is real in mind.**

Also remember we live in a multiverse which has infinite different realities. So you can soften the blow of your team losing by knowing that there are countless other realities where your team won! Let's have a final example of a man watching a movie on TV. A very common and normal thing to do. The normal perspective is that one individual is watching a bunch of actors acting. You will see this differently. What is really happening here? God is watching herself be creative. By making this change in perspective you can still enjoy the movie and also stay rooted in reality.

I have given you just three examples of every-day life. There are of course countless other situations you could come across in this game. But the same basic premise holds for any situation you may find yourself in. **Play the game but know deep down the truth.**

It is worth mentioning at this point that it makes no sense to deny the illusion to the point of not interacting in it. Someone could say that they know life is a computer-generated hologram therefore they are not going to play the game. They might just deny everything around them and just opt out. No, this makes no sense. Yes, it is not real, but we still have to live in this hologram, so it doesn't help you trying to opt out. The answer is to play the game to the best of your ability, enjoy the illusion for what it is but most importantly know deep down the truth that it really is just a game.

So play this game of life. Enjoy it, but as you play, view every single situation you are in through the lens of reality just like I have done for the three examples above. You really can do this yourself. When you view everyday situations from realities point of view it can be enough after a period of time to trigger an enlightenment experience.

You will not be able to predict when an enlightenment experience may happen. What you must do is apply the truth bombs and see every-day situations through the prism of reality and be patient. Don't expect to do this a couple of times and you will be enlightened. No, you will need to have developed a solid habit of seeing reality as it really is. I cannot tell you how long it will take. It may take months or even years of viewing life through realities prism. But I can tell you that an enlightenment experience can hit you at any time. The key is to be kind and patient with yourself and don't give up. You don't need to be perfect at this and you don't need to win every battle with the ego. It would be unrealistic to expect to prevail in every mind attack for example. It is not the end of the world if you succumb to seeing a situation through the lens of the individual person. The key point is just not to give up. If you keep at it, you will eventually become enlightened. What the ego wants is for you to decide "this is all too hard, I can't be bothered with this crap anymore." The ego wants you to go back to your old life. Its job is to remain in full control until you are ready. It is not easy to rise above ego. It takes a sustained effort. But if you desire it enough liberation from suffering can be yours. The key word here is desire. You won't succeed going at this half-hearted. Liberation needs to be your priority. This means putting liberation and freedom from ego above many things in your life.

Where are all the enlightened people in the world?

Most of them are at home living quiet lives. You might think seeing reality as it is, is a pre-requisite for entering politics or law. But no, it isn't. Most enlightened people live quiet, normal lives and the vast majority of politicians operate through ego. Enlightened people still must play in this game in the same way as anyone else. They still have to work, pay taxes and do all the same day to day activities we all do. There is a phrase from Zen Buddhism that says "Before enlightenment chop wood carry water, after enlightenment chop wood carry water." This saying is reminding us that normal day to day life goes on whether you are enlightened or not.

People who are enlightened still have thoughts. They still have negative thoughts. They will still get angry or upset at times. I'm going to say it again so that its crystal clear- people who are enlightened still get angry and upset at times. The only difference is that these negative moments will pass quickly, and they will return to a pleasant feeling of being inherently peaceful and blissful. An enlightened person doesn't have neuroses that bubble away under the surface. But if you think all your life challenges will go away, you would be wrong. Life will still throw you a few curve balls. You could still lose your job. You could become ill. Your house could burn down. But overall, it would be true to say that after enlightenment your life is likely to be much more pleasant and peaceful than it was before. You have returned to the state you were as a baby before you were conditioned by society. You are innately happy, and your suffering has greatly diminished.

It is estimated that there are around 20,000 to 30,000 enlightened souls in the world today. It is hard to be accurate as many enlightened people live quietly and no one can tell by looking at them or even by talking to them. However, this is not a lot of people out of a population of 8 billion people. It works out to be close to .000003% of the world's population. That is roughly three people out of every million. It is a very small amount but it's not surprising because becoming enlightened is not something that is taught in schools. However, by reading this book and applying these truth bombs you have the ability to achieve enlightenment. Your odds are now far better with this book in your hands.

People who have attained enlightenment don't shout it from the rooftops. They don't brag about it for a very simple reason. They are not controlled by their ego. They know they are one with everyone else, so it makes no sense to feel prideful. In a lot of cases if someone is out and about telling everyone who will listen that they are enlightened then they are probably not. It is probably just ego speaking. This would be an example of spiritual ego. In saying this there will be times when it is necessary or helpful for an enlightened person to tell someone else that they are enlightened. So it is not true to say they will never speak of it. It is just they will not say it unnecessarily to pump up their own tyres. That would defeat the whole point. They know that the individual person is not their real identity so why brag about it.

When you attain enlightenment, you will have stopped seeking so you will find you no longer consume spiritual materials like books and YouTube videos so much. You are more likely to want to do things like watching movies or listening to music. You may enjoy walking and being in nature. The classic stereotype of an enlightened monk living alone in a cave is one possible way to live, but there are a million different ways enlightened people live. They can be anybody and outwardly you would probably not know unless you knew them very well. Even then you might not know and just think that they are very calm and peaceful.

Many people from the west have very little knowledge of what enlightenment even means. If it was valued by society as much as say becoming wealthy was, then we would see many more souls achieving it. It is explained and taught by many of the Eastern religions however including Buddhism, Confucianism and Hinduism. Most people living in the west have very little knowledge of the basics of these eastern religions. They know much more about Christianity, and this is very different to these eastern religions. Christianity does not teach about enlightenment even though Jesus Christ was clearly an enlightened being. In fact, many scholars and spiritual teachers believe that Jesus undertook a pilgrimage in his life and that he travelled to the East in search of knowledge. Christianity does not even teach about basic spiritual truths like re-incarnation. It is no wonder so few have attained enlightenment given this lack of knowledge of even what it is.

The knowledge that one gains from becoming enlightened is not common knowledge. The content of this book is certainly not common knowledge. Enlightened people are not out there espousing the truths that are in this book to everyone they come across. If I was to start telling random people in the west that they are God and that the world is an illusion, they would look at me very strangely. They may suspect I was delusional. However, if I said this to someone from the east they would say "of course." There may come a time in the future where the content in this book is indeed common knowledge. There may come a tipping point once a critical mass or number of people know the truth. Right now, in 2023 many people do not know this truth. There are many books and YouTube videos saying the same things I am saying here. Despite this, that tipping point has not been reached.

If you are in an argument with someone it will not serve you to tell that person that they don't exist as a person and that they are just a hologram. You will learn to keep this knowledge to yourself unless you believe the other person is ready for you to drop them a seed of truth. You will be considered insane by many people if you espouse this content to them but the irony of this is that you are the sane one living in an insane world. The great spiritual teacher Eckhart Tolle has said that the world is insane and the reason it is insane is because almost everybody is living in ego. The nature of ego is insanity. Remember ego is a kind of operating system we use to interact with each other. The world is using an operating system which is rooted in insanity. This is just a reflection of where we are as a species.

Don't be saddened by this state of affairs. This is where we are meant to be as a species right now. Ego serves a function for a while until we outgrow it. You have an amazing opportunity as an individual to transcend living with an ego operating system. This is how we will evolve as a species. One by one.

Meditation helps us ignore negative thoughts

We have discussed earlier in the book that thoughts are like clouds, in that they come and go. We do not want to get attached to our thoughts. Most thoughts delude us into thinking we are an ego. Every time we have the "I" thought or the "me" thought we are being lured into thinking we are a person. What we want to do is to develop a separation from our thoughts. We must realise that we are a presence which is just listening in to these thoughts. Our essence is not these thoughts. Pay no attention to any thoughts that bother you. Don't fight against them, just let them be. Fighting against them or resisting them just makes them more real.

That is where meditation helps. The more we meditate the clearer this becomes. You do not need to meditate for hours at a time, and you do not need to be perfect at it. Even if you only meditate for 5 minutes a day it will still help but twenty minutes a day is the magic number. Twenty minutes once a day will give you real and lasting benefits. Any type of meditation is good. I have heard many people say "I am useless at meditation." or "my mind is too busy for me to meditate." Just do your best. Again, you do not need to be perfect at it. Do not have expectations of stopping all your thoughts because that is impossible. You will have a jumble of thoughts so just let the thoughts come and go and concentrate on your breathing.

Meditation is for the mind as exercise is for the body. It is really important. Develop a meditation habit. Find a time slot of twenty minutes in your day and make that meditation time and use that same time slot every day. They say it takes three weeks to create a habit. So, try for three weeks so that you can establish a habit. Meditation calms the mind, and it helps you get in contact with the stillness which is the "I am." I can't stress enough just how useful meditation is in your spiritual development. It will also increase your levels of happiness.

Here is a simple and very effective method of meditation. It is called the breathing method with a twist that helps make it easier. Sit or lie comfortably and close your eyes. Breathe in a long steady breath through your mouth. This may take about 3 seconds. As you breathe in, visualise a line of white smoke going down your body from the mouth all the way down to your toes. By visualising this smoke your attention will naturally be on the inside of your body and not on your thoughts. Just ignore any thoughts that come to mind because they will come. You do this with the inbreath. Now breathe out that breath through your nose. The outbreath should also be about 3 seconds (you can shorten this if you wish). With this outbreath visualise black soot coming out of your nose. That's it. You just repeat this process over and over for 20 minutes.

Summary of truth bombs

I would like to finish this chapter by summarising the truth bombs that we have learnt. It would be great if you could become familiar with each one. They are very powerful and when used they can totally change the way you see a certain situation. Remember that being enlightened just means that you see reality as it really is. That is all it is. Rather than seeing through the lens of ego you see through the prism of reality.

Truth Bomb 1: *We are a divine soul made of divine consciousness.*

Truth Bomb 2: *We are the entire universe and everything in the universe is one.*

Truth Bomb 3: *We create our own reality, and everything happens for a good reason.*

Truth Bomb 4: *Everything we see around us is an illusion. Everything, including our bodies is a holographic projection.*

Truth Bomb 5: *You are that other person, and they are you.*

Truth Bomb 6: *Every person I see is really God.*

Truth Bomb 7: *Life is not real.*

Truth Bomb 8: *I have no free will, life simply unfolds by itself.*

Take a photo of these truth bombs and keep it on your phone. You can refer to the photo at random throughout each day until you have committed them to memory. This is not just a trick to confuse the ego, this is reality. Knowing and believing that these truth bombs are true increases their potency.

If you find yourself in a situation where you are experiencing emotional suffering, ask yourself; why am I suffering? What is it about this situation that is making me suffer? Then ask yourself, **which one or more of these truth bombs will provide the antidote to the suffering I am feeling**? Then look at the situation through the prism of these truth bombs. When you do this, you are seeing reality as it really is.

When you see the true reality of any situation you free yourself from self-recriminations and negativity. It is not necessary to emotionally suffer in life. You can free yourself from self-blame. You can avoid having negative emotions towards others. You do this by simply seeing what is really happening. What is the reality of the situation? These truth bombs make up the prism through which you can now view life. I can promise you that if you do this your life will become immeasurably better. You will believe these truths more and more until you reach the point where you transcend the belief you are an ego and become spiritually enlightened.

You have been playing this game a long time now without even understanding the basic aspects to the game. It's like you have been playing with a blind fold on. Once you have memorised the truth bombs above at least you will finally understand the way this game works. You can expect far better results. It's like an American football star playing rugby for the first time with no knowledge of the rules. How do you think he's going to go? Probably not too great. That's what you have been doing up till now. Playing a game without a proper knowledge of the rules and laws of the game. How can you expect to shine when you are in a situation like this?

I explained earlier how sudden awakening or sudden enlightenment unfolds. Now I will explain how the more common gradual awakening or gradual enlightenment occurs.

What will happen first is the mind starts to quiet down over time. You will find its not bothering you with as many negative thought loops. Your mind won't be taking you back into the past worrying over things that happened long ago. It will not be projecting into the future so often and causing you so much anxiety.

You will start to feel moments of bliss that come and go. You will love this new feeling of bliss! It's hard to explain what it feels like to someone who is not enlightened. To be totally honest the closest thing I can think of is that it feels similar to the affects you feel after taking a drug like MDMA or ecstasy. It does not feel exactly like this as it feels more subtle than ecstasy but it's the closest thing I can think of. Of course, unlike ecstasy there is absolutely no come down.

As well as the bliss coming and going you will realise that you are feeling much more peaceful. You are getting to the point where you are at peace with the world. You are not so attached to things going the way you want them too. You slowly over time surrender to what is. You accept whatever it is that is showing up in your life. If life throws you a few curve balls you don't resist, you just accept that this thing has happened and feel happy anyway. This all happens gradually.

To start with you feel bliss for short periods of time. Over time these short blissful moments happen more frequently. While this is happening you will be learning not to be so attached to certain outcomes or aspects of your life. **You start to feel that everything is actually okay just the way it is.** This feeling gets stronger and stronger. Even life altering change or severe shocks to your way of life no longer have the power to upset you. You become like a coconut tree which sways in the middle of a storm. You go with the flow. You don't resist. This is a huge jump in your evolution. You accept life just the way it is and you don't get upset. This is the most common form of Enlightenment. This is true happiness.

When you get there you will laugh. For sure you will laugh out loud. It doesn't seem funny now but trust me once you get a taste of enlightenment it is hilarious. It seems so obvious and you laugh because you can hardly believe the way you used to view yourself and the way you viewed the universe.

You will be naturally calm most of the time, not because nothing goes wrong, but because nothing feels personal anymore. There is a quiet happiness and contentment just being alive, even doing ordinary stuff like making coffee or going for a walk. Problems still show up but they don't stick. They pass without the old stress, fear or drama. You feel more loving, more present, and oddly free, like you've finally relaxed into being exactly what you already were.

Does this feel like something you would like to experience? You can have this for yourself. You can finally let go of personhood and have all this. This book can get you there but there is so much more information online. So you must seek out that information. It's there on the internet, YouTube, in books and even AI can be a massive help. AI has access to the highest truths from the great spiritual teachers. All of this is at your finger-tips. You can do this!

Chapter 5
The Meaning of Life

Introduction

Ever since I was a young boy I have wondered "Why am I here?" "What is the point of living this life?" "Why is there something rather than nothing?" I have never understood why this is so rarely discussed or talked about. I remember as a child watching the Monty Python film, "The Meaning of Life," thinking "great, I'm going to finally find out why I'm here." How disappointing to find out it was a comedy that didn't address the question at all. More disappointment was to come after I found out that the book "Hitchhikers Guide to the Galaxy" also covered the topic of the meaning of life. In this book the answer to the meaning of life, the universe, and everything was simply the number 42. I was left feeling cheated again.

Have you ever pondered these questions? Have you ever wondered what caused the big bang? Or what was there before the big bang? All we know is that we are conscious and alive right now, but we are not taught how we fit in with the divine plan. In this chapter I am going to tell you exactly what the divine game we are playing right now is. I will explain how it works. You will know why you are here and where you will go in future lives. It is possible to answer these questions. I know because I have found the answers which I will share with you here in this chapter.

You are here on this Earth because this planet and the other souls here are a match for where your soul is at. If you were more evolved, you wouldn't be here. You would be on a planet with other souls who are more evolved than those here on Earth. You have an opportunity to evolve higher in this life so that your next life will be on a higher-level planet. In this chapter I will outline what is ahead for you. **The game has a hierarchical**

structure. It is organised in such a way so that souls are grouped together with other souls who are at the same level in terms of how evolved they are.

I will list the different levels there are in the game and I will explain each level. I will tell you how long an incarnation at each level will last for. For example, in this life you can expect to live for 80 years but once you jump one level higher the average life span for an incarnation is 90,000 years. When you get to three levels higher you can expect each incarnation to last 75 million years. There is a reason why this life you are leading is so much shorter than lives at the higher levels. It is because this level which is largely about overcoming ego is considered by far the hardest level.

When you get one level higher than you are now you will have a combination of a chemical and light body. One level higher again and your entire body is made of light.

This level has 100 times more suffering involved in it than the next level. Lifespans are short in this level to get it over with quickly. No soul enjoys suffering but the suffering is necessary to help you look within and seek so that you can become enlightened and overcome ego. The lives ahead for you past this level will be far more enjoyable.

I will also explain the powers you will have in the higher levels. For example, at one level higher than you are now you will learn to communicate telepathically. Once your soul progresses two levels higher it will be able to **travel by teleportation and you will be able to manipulate consciousness and create matter out of thought.** This is all just an introduction about what I will break down at the end of this chapter. Rest assured there is a divine plan that is taking place in this game right now it is just that you are only seeing one level of it. There is much more to come. Before I break down all the details of future lives, I want to return to what the meaning is for this life. The life you are living now.

Various spiritual teachers do touch upon meaning in life but there does not seem to be a straight answer that everyone can agree on. I want to be very upfront about what I personally believe the meaning of playing this computer game is. I have realised that there is more than just one meaning to life. There are several meanings, and I am going to list them all and then explain each one. It makes sense that there is more than just one meaning. Having multiple benefits is always better than having just one.

I need to start with a disclaimer that these meanings are only my opinion. Different spiritual teachers will always have different beliefs. I am basing my beliefs here on a near lifetime of searching and decades of reading and research. These are all big picture beliefs. What this means is that these meanings to life are from the perspective of the soul. These are objectives your soul would have had moments before it uploaded itself into this game.

The meaning of life

Let's get straight to it. Let's create a list.
- To simply experience everything there is to experience.
- To learn (or remember) specific lessons so that the soul can grow in love and wisdom.
- To achieve a specific goal or a legacy to benefit the world.
- To become spiritually enlightened.
- To return to our natural state of perfect happiness.
- Whatever meaning you want it to be.
- To choose between service to self or service to others.

To simply experience all there is to experience

This is what God wants. This is why God created this computer simulation and split himself up into a vast number of souls and uploaded them into the game. As I mentioned in the beginning of this book God wanted to experience more than just love, bliss and perfect happiness. He wanted to experience every possible situation there could ever be. Every emotion there could ever be.

This extraordinary game delivers exactly this. Limitless experiences. Every possible thing that could happen is happening in the multiverse right now. I can say this with confidence because the multiverse is infinite in size and there are possibly infinite parallel realities. Let's take this reality we are in now. We believe that beyond the observable universe that the universe stretches on forever. There are likely countless other forms of life. Different species ranging from highly evolved beings down to a vast array of rudimentary life. There are things happening in the universe beyond our ability to see that we cannot even imagine. God gets to experience all of this. Can you see just how perfect this extraordinary game really is?

The beauty of this game is that it is a social one. We get to interact with each other. That is what makes it so interesting. Before God split himself up, he might have been a little bored at times. Not now. There are so many souls in an infinite universe. There is so much happening. Anything that can

happen is happening and God gets to experience all of it. Some of these
things, humans might label as bad or even evil. God doesn't care about that.
God wants to experience contrast and that means good and evil, joyful and
sad, exciting and mundane. Everything is valid. God gets to experience all of
it!

**To learn (or remember) specific lessons so that the soul can grow in love
and wisdom**

This game is like school. It's a place of learning where we learn spiritual
lessons. It's the perfect place to grow and evolve. I mention "learning
lessons" several times in the book but strictly speaking we are not really
learning lessons. We are more correctly "remembering lessons." This is
because the soul already understands all this stuff, but it chooses to
temporarily forget it all so that it can incarnate in the game and so that the
game will work properly. As it goes through each of its incarnations it can
remember each lesson one by one. However, I speak of learning lessons in
this book because of the simplicity of this concept and because this is how it
seems from the perspective of the reader.

We all can think about our own life and pinpoint lessons we have learnt in
the past. Often learning lessons is painful. Sometimes it's when life seems to
go to pieces that we get that harsh lesson. This is a good thing. We are better
for it. Often these lessons involve other souls. This computer game we are
playing is a social one. It's kind of like a social experiment. The things we say
and do to other people sometimes elicit a different reaction than we
anticipate and thus we learn. It's through these relationships with other
people that we grow.

The lessons we learn often add to our level of wisdom. Those wise souls
we see among us have often gained their wisdom through experience. You
have heard the term "old soul." These old souls have probably had more
incarnations than most and this is why they seem to have such good
judgement and just seem to know things that others may not be able to see
or understand. There is a direct link between learning lessons and wisdom.
The more lessons we learn the wiser we become.

Love and wisdom are two pillars of spirituality. Love is the feminine
aspect. Christianity focuses mainly on this aspect of love. It does this very
well. Examples of this include the way Christians speak of the love of Christ.
Also, the devotion and veneration Christians show to Mary is another
example of the emphasis Christians place on love. Wisdom on the other

hand is the masculine aspect and the eastern religions like Hinduism, Confucianism and Buddhism focus heavily on this. Examples of this include the way Buddhism breaks down spirituality into steps and paths. It uses terms like "attachments and fetters." These are concepts one can use to measure how advanced one's spiritual development is. The emphasis of Eastern religions is not about becoming more loving but instead about overcoming emotional suffering. You can see that Western religions are very different to Eastern religions. Neither is better than the other. Both are equal. All souls hope that at the end of their incarnation they have grown in both love and wisdom.

We may have some very specific goals which our soul has targeted the moment it started planning out its life. Here are a few examples of possible goals:

- To open up to others.
- To be selfless.
- To live with integrity.
- To be honest.
- To love oneself.
- To stop caring what others think of oneself

The definition of wisdom is "the quality of having experience, knowledge and good judgement." Most of us will agree that as we get older, we improve in this quality. This is only one life we are living here. We can only get so much wisdom from one incarnation, but we must remember we are immortal and have many incarnations ahead of us. The sky is the proverbial limit and there is no rush. When your body dies the soul will conduct a life review where it will look back at the life just lived and ascertain whether those wisdom goals have been met. Hopefully they will be met but if they are not, no problem, you just need to re-set and try again in another incarnation.

Many of the lessons we learn come from making mistakes and of course we all make them. I have made some beauties. But the good news is that it doesn't matter how bad or how big your mistakes are because you learn and gain wisdom from them. So, from this perspective your biggest mistakes have been really valuable, and they have helped you. If you are inclined to look back in the past and ruminate on past mistakes at least comfort yourself with the knowledge your mistakes were very valuable to you.

There is one other benefit from making mistakes and learning lessons. When we make each mistake, we usually experience some suffering at the time e.g., anger, shame, or embarrassment. I mentioned earlier in the book that suffering eventually leads people to look within and wake up. Using this logic, you could say that the more mistakes you make the better. More mistakes mean more suffering and more suffering means the more you look deeply inwards and the more likely you are to have a spiritual awakening and follow the spiritual path. This is why mistakes are so valuable. Imagine if you never made any mistakes. You might have some fun, but you wouldn't grow in wisdom and evolve into a better version of yourself. You would also never wake up and follow the spiritual path.

Before you incarnated into the game, it's possible that your soul had one or two really big lessons it wished to remember. This may have been a big part of the whole reason to incarnate. It wanted to remember these lessons so it could grow and evolve. Its best to look at your mistakes in life from this perspective. The soul's perspective.

To achieve a specific goal or a legacy to benefit the world

Every soul that incarnates into the game has several specific goals it wishes to achieve during its incarnation. We can say that these goals are part of the meaning of your life. Every soul wishes to evolve higher and higher with each incarnation. They wish to build upon their spiritual achievements already achieved. Have you ever wondered if there is one thing that is your destiny? Is there something you feel you are meant to achieve in this life? Perhaps there is. Perhaps you are here on a mission. Perhaps before incarnating into the game your soul had a specific plan to do something here on Earth and leave a legacy for all that follow. If so, then we must say this is a big part of the overall meaning of your life.

Is there something you have always wanted to do but haven't because of fear? It could be fear of failure or fear of the unknown. It could even be fear of success. Are you playing it safe in life? Doing what you have always done? Is there a different or new trajectory your life could take? For many, the answer to these questions is yes. It usually just takes some courage to follow our heart and do that which we are meant to do. Using courage does not mean we feel bullet proof. When we use courage, we are usually very fearful and that is exactly why we need the courage to get us through.

How do we know what it is that we are meant to do? This is actually an easy question to answer. It's the thing that we love doing. The thing that brings us joy. In other words, it's our passion. When we devote time to our passions, we are doing what we love. If we can make a career out of doing what we love, we have found ourselves the perfect job. There are so many people stuck in jobs that they hate. It is only a few who are living their dreams by making a career out of doing what they love.

Let's look at some souls who have left a legacy here in this game for all who will follow. Imagine if Mick Jagger had worked in administration his whole life. The world would be without his music. What if Steve Jobs went into accountancy instead of creating the iPad and iPhone. Sometimes following your passions may not bring joy but it may bring inner fulfillment. Imagine if Mother Theresa had gone into a clerical position rather than helping the poorest of the poor. Or if the great Nelson Mandela had never taken a stance on his political and social justice beliefs. There is nothing wrong with accountancy and clerical work by the way. For some people this may be their passion and they will get much satisfaction and enjoyment from it. That is the whole point. We are all different. What is appealing for someone may be horrible for someone else. **We can all fail at doing what we hate so we may as well take a chance at succeeding at something we love.**

In my life I have had a number of jobs. It has taken me fifty years to finally be happy and joyful working two casual jobs. My point is that it can take quite a long time to find your truth. Some of you may find it very quickly while for others it may take several decades. This is my list of jobs I have had; milk truck driver and delivery, hotel porter, wine steward, barman, high school teacher, tutor, special school teacher, real estate agent, Airbnb operator, interviewer. Some of these jobs I enjoyed more than others, but I can't say I loved all of them.

With my AirBnB work and my interviewer work I actually want to spend time doing these things. It brings me pleasure and that is the key. This is the question you must ask yourself. What is it that you love doing? Then find a way to do it. My two jobs are not high level but I'm fine with that. This work is not the legacy I will leave once I return home. My legacy will be this book and the people who I have helped by writing this book.

THE MEANING OF LIFE

There are many examples of people from our history leaving a legacy. The common denominator amongst them all is that they all used courage to go for it. They embraced their passions and made their passions their life work. People like Albert Einstein, Nelson Mandela, William Shakespeare, Aristotle, Isaac Newton, Mother Teresa, Henry Ford, the Wright Brothers, Steve Jobs, Marie Curie. These people left a legacy. They changed the world and made good on the intentions of their soul during their time playing this game. Not only did these people follow their passions, they did it for the benefit of the world not just for themselves. This is the ultimate way to leave a legacy because you are doing something good for everyone else playing the game.

To become spiritually enlightened

Making the shift from being a slave to your ego to living in reality is the biggest individual achievement we can make in life. It is a watershed moment. It marks a large and significant advance in our spiritual evolution. As I have said throughout this book you are already God, and you can't do much better than that. The problem is you don't realise it. Enlightenment is living out this truth. Everyone gets there in the end. It is impossible not to. So why not make it this lifetime to make the shift in consciousness that is required.

Buddhism tells us that when we reach enlightenment it frees us from the cycle of suffering and rebirth. This means our next incarnation will not be here on Earth. We move onwards to a planet with a higher level of evolution. For those of us saddened by the state of our world, this makes for an appealing change.

There is no reason why you cannot achieve the state of enlightenment in this life. I have written Chapter 4 in such a way as to give you a road map to enlightenment. By following and practicing the steps outlined in this chapter any one can succeed in going the whole way. Holding those truth bombs in your awareness as you go about your day is the key. You are ready to make this shift and it's really up to you as to whether you want to continue to live in a holographic illusion and believe it is all real or whether you want to live in reality.

Three keys that will get you there are the attributes of **perseverance, patience and desire to be free of suffering.** Desire is the main quality needed. You must have a burning desire to be free of suffering. I am at the point now that whenever my mind gives me something painful to think about, I just refuse to listen. I have had enough suffering in my life so I say "no more" and I just let that thought from the mind pass. I refuse to engage with it no matter how painful it is. This is what you need to do too. Do not be allured by old memories or painful thoughts. When they come up you have two choices. 1. To be sucked into mulling over the pain. 2. Let the thoughts and memories pass. Take a stand like I do. **Draw a line in the sand right now**. No more suffering. Refuse to suffer anymore.

Just keep at it. See reality as it really is. Don't give up because at some point it is all going to click for you. You will feel a wave of bliss just sweep through your mind and body. This will happen when you really and truly believe in reality. It will be a beautiful moment in your life but it may take some time so that is why patience is necessary. But you can do this. So, support yourself along the way. Don't be hard on yourself, just give it your best shot applying the truth bombs. I can promise you that at some point the belief will really kick in and you will finally experience the bliss which is your birthright.

To return to our natural state of perfect happiness

Many spiritual teachers quite rightly say the meaning of life is to find happiness. The only way to find true and long-lasting happiness is to achieve the state of spiritual enlightenment as explained above. There is nothing we need to add to ourselves to find happiness. In fact, it's the opposite. It is a process of stripping away. We must strip away layers of illusion. Many of these layers of illusion come from societal conditioning. We get it from our parents firstly and then from society in general. It can be painful stripping away these falsehoods, but it is necessary. We were born onto this Earth perfect and perfectly happy. We must strip away until we have stripped everything away and return to that original state.

Be patient with yourself. You have spent a lifetime of taking onboard conditioning so don't expect to clear it all in five minutes. It will take time. The spiritual teacher Rupert Spira is spot on with his analogy of going to bed at night after removing all of your clothes. He has said that clothes are like the layers of conditioning you have. When you have removed all your clothes you stand there naked before getting into bed. The naked body represents a soul stripped away of all conditioning.

You may be wondering what is this conditioning exactly? It is basically anything and everything you believe about the personal individual self you appear to be. Here are some common forms of conditioning many of us have come to believe is true:

- − I am unworthy.
- − I should try to please other people.
- − I need to be liked by others.
- − My body is not good enough.
- − Money is hard to come by.

There are limitless pieces of conditioning we have come to believe. So, it takes time to strip all of it away. **The stripping away of many of these pieces of conditioning happens naturally as a result of personal growth**. Getting into personal development accelerates this natural process.

The process I outline in the appendix of this book deals with limiting beliefs, and it is another way to remove conditioning. It will help you remove some of these pieces of conditioning from your subconscious mind. It only takes about one minute to remove a limiting belief using this process. Conditioning and limiting beliefs are often the same thing. This process is very quick, very easy and highly effective.

Feeling happy is all any of us can ever want. It is one of the greatest achievements we can get from life. Imagine if every morning when you wake up you just felt so very happy that another day is beginning, and that happiness stayed with you all day until you lay down at night. What more can you want than that? Just being happy and loving life. This happiness goes hand in hand with spiritual enlightenment. Achieving the state of enlightenment instantly gives you happiness. It cuts through all the conditioning and negative beliefs. This is the fast track to happiness. In fact, this is the only way to have real and sustained happiness because it's the only way to overcome suffering. If you are not enlightened, you can still increase your happiness levels using the ideas I outlined earlier in the section on unconditional happiness in Chapter 1.

Whatever meaning you want it to be
Very simply the meaning of life is whatever you want it to be. You are in charge of your life. You can decide what the meaning of it is.

This will obviously be different for everyone, and it might change as you go through different stages of your life. It helps to have your own meaning or else it's hard to get out of bed in the morning. I know myself, this meaning that I personally give to life has changed a lot as I've got older. For me it's often been tied to the occupation I have been in. As I look back now these are some of the things in life that gave me meaning.

Attending university, my goals were very simple. I wanted to successfully get a degree in economics and marketing. This was the main goal, but I had other purposes in my life which was all about enjoying alcohol, parties and girls. My life at this time was very social. I had left home for the first time, so I had all these new-found freedoms. So, this was a time when everything felt brand new. I was free from my parents for the first time and loving it.

I did bar work in London and New Zealand after I finished university. Now having achieved my degree my purpose remained very social. It was basically pubs, alcohol and still girls. Living in London was a very exciting time for me. It was so much bigger and there was so much more going on than the city I came from in New Zealand. This was a time in my life that was simply about having fun.

I started doing high school teaching at age 27 back in New Zealand and my goals changed then. My meaning to life was to be the best teacher of economics and accounting I could be. I wanted simply to be a good teacher. I believe I did achieve this. I enjoyed economics in particular and found the teaching of it to be very rewarding. I wanted to inspire the kids I was teaching to become really interested in economics and to understand how economics relates to the level of prosperity citizens of a country enjoy.

At this time, I also discovered electronic music and the rave scene in Auckland, New Zealand. Every Friday night for two years I would go out dancing with my partner (now wife Karyn) and friends. We would go to night clubs and dance parties and literally dance all night. We took recreational drugs to enhance the experience. Mainly amphetamines (speed). I didn't realise it at the time, but this was actually a spiritual experience for me. I loved it. I would look forward to this all week. I must say that at this time in my life, a big meaning to life that I held was dancing all night to electronic music and feeling my spirit soar while I lost myself in the music. I can remember dancing and feeling so ecstatic one time that I repeated the Our Father prayer to source while dancing with an incredible feeling of gratitude and pure joy.

This all sounds good but I experienced very real come downs which lasted days. There are dangers using drugs like these and I do not recommend that you take psychedelics or any other form of drugs. The choice was mine and I chose to use them. If you do decide to take drugs especially psychedelics you can make spiritual gains but you can also have a very fearful and terrifying experience too. So I recommend that you do your research.

In my mid 30's I moved into the teaching of children in special school settings. My meaning then was more about helping children with learning problems or intellectual disabilities. Many of the students had autism. I wanted to give these kids life skills to help them once they left school. I found teaching special kids was not as rewarding as high school teaching. This was because the special kids learn quite slowly so I had to be very patient. I did this form of teaching for over a decade.

I decided on a career change in my late 40's. I left teaching behind and decided to have a go at being a real estate agent. This was something I always wanted to do. At this time the meaning to my life was largely about money and selling as much real estate as I could. Some people may see the pursuit of money to be the root of all evil, but it is not. Money is a neutral energy. It can be used for both good and bad. Money can buy flowers and it can also buy weapons of war. There is nothing inherently bad about money. The more money you have in your life the more freedom you have and the more good deeds you can do in the game. This vision of being a real estate highflyer was what got me out of bed each morning. However, I wasn't really cut out for real estate. I think I sold about 25 houses in three years. It wasn't really enough to make a good living out of. So, after three years I left that behind too.

These things were obviously career based but I had other meaning in my life which was just as important, in fact more important. My family has always been and always will be very important to me. I have been in a relationship with my wife for over 20 years and she has been rock-solid and a beautiful partner for me. I call her my angel. She is incredible.

I had a spiritual awakening in my 40's and had a period (about 8 years) of spiritual seeking where my own spiritual development was far more important to me than any of the career-based goals I have already mentioned like real estate. I had the drive, the determination and the desire to find the answers to the big questions. I hunted for material on the internet and YouTube to learn from the great spiritual teachers. I read many books. I was now a very different person to the one a decade ago. My goal was to find out what the meaning of life really was.

Right now, I have meaning which comes from being an author of this book. I want to publish this book and I hope it will help at least 1000 people within 3 years. I have heard the expression that people often say which is "If I help just one person it will be worth it." I hope to do better than one person, so I have decided that a goal of helping 1000 people is a good number.

That is an honest list of the meaning I have had in my life up until now. I have no doubt that this will change again as I get older. Some people might have much more specific goals than mine and they may well have much bigger and more grandiose goals than these. For others, the goals could be something family oriented like being a good mum or dad.

There is no right or wrong with this. Your meaning may be vastly different to what I have shared. Whatever it is, it's perfect. Once again, your emotions are a good barometer of how suitable your current goals are. If you are working away at your meaning to life and you find your emotions are negative, then you know that something needs to change. I have mentioned earlier in the book that turning your passion into your life's work is the key. The ultimate is being paid for doing what you love. That may not be possible, but you may still be able to engage in your passion and get money from a different job that you work at part time. Currently I earn money from operating an Airbnb business. Or even better you could have a passive income stream which allows you to do what you love.

I am currently happier than I have ever been in my life. I have my Airbnb business and I also work as an interviewer and this allows me to meet all sorts of different people. I actually love doing this job. But it has taken me 50 years to finally do what I love. I hope that you may find out what your truth is and that it does not take as long. But even if it takes 80 years it doesn't matter because you have got there in the end.

To choose between service to self or service to others

I am now going to introduce you to some incredible knowledge that is not well known which amongst other things explains the hierarchical structure of the game. If you have ever wondered "what is actually going on here?" You are about to find out. This section of the book is based on information from a highly evolved being from another species and planet. This being is known as Ra and he was channelled by spiritualists/mediums in the 1980's. The three individuals who channelled this incredible information were Don Elkins, Jim McCarty and Carla Rueckert.

The information gained from Ra is known as "The Law of One Material." **In it he literally describes to us how the game works. It is incredible information that tells us the order and hierarchical structure of the game.**

He explains how life is grouped together depending on how evolved it is.
Ra explained that every planet in the game has a classification including
Earth. He also explained that all lifeforms are classified based on how
evolved they are. All life is classified into one of seven densities. **They are
classified on a scale of one to seven densities with first density being the
least evolved and seventh density being the highest evolved.** Our Earth is
considered a third/fourth density planet and the human beings on Earth at
this time are also classified as either third density or fourth density beings.
This means that most people on Earth are classified as third density and
some have graduated to fourth density. Ra himself is a sixth density being.
Seventh density is the last stage which precedes returning to and merging
back with divine source (the glorious end of the game).

Do you sometimes despair at the state of the world? I'm talking about
wars that are currently taking place. I have never known world peace in my
lifetime. There are millions of starving children in various parts of the world.
Homelessness in cities all over the world.

Well this is what you get when a planet is inhabited by mainly third
density souls. This is very simply where we are at in terms of how evolved we
are. You are here on this planet because your soul vibrates and resonates at
this level. So, if you wish to be in a better world then you need to evolve and
become a better version of yourself. If you do this then your next lifetime
may be on a planet where poverty and wars are unheard of. Does this sound
good? It's a great incentive to work on yourself. Focus on being more loving,
more selfless, be kinder, be generous, show more empathy. Do these things.
Focus on these things rather than focusing on yourself or on becoming rich
or famous.

You may be wondering what is the difference between third density souls
and fourth density souls. You may be wondering what specific density you
are yourself. There's actually a very precise way this is determined. To
graduate from third density to the higher fourth density you must complete
a process known as **"The Choosing."**

One of the things that third density beings like many of us on Earth must
do is what Ra calls **"The Choosing."** The choosing is something we do
throughout this life and other incarnations on third density worlds. We are
choosing one of two options or two polarities; **service to self or service to
others.** Service to self is all about helping yourself at all costs. It is a selfish
way to live. You are looking out for number one. Service to others is all about

helping other souls. It is a selfless way to live. You are actively giving of yourself for the benefit of others.

Ra explained that we do this choosing through our thoughts, words and deeds. When we help that homeless person or mow our neighbor's lawn, we are choosing service to others. When we extort others through something like profiteering, we are choosing service to self. This decision is not an instant one. It depends on how you live over a number of lifetimes. The good deeds and bad deeds all count, and they will all be factored in to determine which polarity you are matching. The choice either way will be a reflection of the way you have lived your third density lives. If the majority of your actions have been selfless, you will be determined as a soul wanting service to others.

On the other hand, if most of your deeds have been selfish, then you will be determined as a soul wanting service to self. If you decide you wish to explore service to self, it is harder to achieve than service to others. You will need to make at least 95% of your actions selfish ones to succeed. By contrast if you want to explore service to others, you will need to make at least 51% of your actions selfless ones. **You must finish the choosing before you can graduate from third density to fourth density.**

As I mentioned you may be wondering what density you are yourself. There is no way to be certain that you have finished the choosing and have graduated to fourth density. All you can go on is your intuition. However, now that you know about the choosing, you can consciously go out into the world and do deeds which align with either service to self or service to others. It is your choice which option to work towards. It may be that you want to explore service to self. If this is what you want, then to graduate you can selfishly look out for number one. Your actions will be self-centered, and you will not care about anyone else but yourself. On the other hand, you may prefer the idea of service to others, then to graduate you will consciously go out into the world with a selfless attitude and do good deeds for others.

You may be wondering if its possible to choose service to self and still become enlightened. The answer is yes, it's possible. Becoming enlightened is simply about seeing reality. You can see the truth of reality and still be selfish at the human level. I think it would be harder to achieve but yes, it is possible. If this sounds like something you would like to try then I wish you good luck. It is not for others to judge and source herself has no problem with it at all.

Most beings in the game eventually choose service to others which is also called the positive polarity. A smaller number choose service to self which is also called the negative polarity. Ra makes clear that **no one polarity is better or worse than another.** This means that if you choose service to self this is just as acceptable as service to others. Ra gave an example of an infamous individual from Earth's history who continued to choose the negative polarity or service to self. His name was Grigori Rasputin. Google describes Rasputin as follows, *"A sexual deviant, mystic healer, political saboteur and renegade monk."* Others described him as being pure evil. From source's point of view Rasputin is just as loved and his life just as valid as anyone choosing service to others.

God has no prerequisite for what you choose. He wishes to experience everything including what we call evil. If you do choose the negative polarity however, you can only do it up to sixth density. The reason is because by the time you get to the verge of a seventh density life (the highest density) you will be forced to reverse your polarity to continue on. However, souls can and do choose service to self for many lifetimes.

With this in mind, we can now add choosing a polarity as one of the meanings of our life.

I would like to expand on the law of one material. This channelled material from the 1980's gives us a massive **insight into reality**. It serves as providing answers to many big questions like **what the heck is going on here?** I will start by explaining how we graduate up through the densities as we go from one incarnation to another. It takes thousands of lifetimes to get through all the densities. When we have finally reached the end (finishing seventh density lifetimes) we merge back to divine source. No one can know what this may feel like, but we can guess that it would be breathtaking and majestic. We become the supreme creator in all her full glory and power. We know everything and have the power to do anything. We are pure love and light. **We exist as the supreme God for a period of time** until we eventually decide to split from source once more and form a new soul. We start the cycle all over again as a first density soul in a **completely new** and **completely different game** and start working our way up once more. It is like this for infinity! **This is how life works.**

Seven densities of life

Let's look at each density and list the characteristic of each one. As we progress through the densities our vibrational rate increases. We are almost always growing and evolving forward with each incarnation. I would like to thank the great spiritual teacher Aaron Abke for introducing me to this material through his YouTube channel and in particular his video "The Seven Densities of Consciousness." I also thank the lawofonesociety.com website for the vast information which is on this website. The information below comes from these sources. I encourage anyone who finds this information interesting to visit this website or to subscribe to Aaron Abke's YouTube channel.

As I describe the densities, I am describing the level of evolution of the souls at each level. For example, Earth is a third/fourth density planet. This means that the souls who have incarnated here as humans are either third density souls or fourth density souls. Those souls here on Earth that have graduated to fourth density have only just tipped over into this density. It will take many incarnations and millions of years until they develop all the qualities of an established fourth density being. Jesus Christ was an established fourth density being when he incarnated on Earth in the first century. We can see that there is the potential for massive spiritual growth in the fourth density alone. Later fourth density beings like Jesus often form what is called a social memory complex. This means that they form small groups and actually join minds. They have a combination of what is called a light body and a chemical body, and their communication is telepathic.

The planet Earth has only just graduated to fourth density. The planet itself has a spiritual vibration which matches that of the souls who have incarnated here. It has been a third density planet up until the year 2012 at which time it graduated to fourth density as foreseen by the Mayan civilisation. During the year 2012 there was a tipping point reached. The overall vibration of the souls here on this Earth increased enough to tip the scales of balance over into the higher fourth density.

As the spiritual vibration of the souls here on Earth continues to evolve and grow so does the vibration of the planet Earth itself. If you are wondering what density other lifeforms on our planet are. The animals on Earth are second density souls. Plants and microbial life are also second density. Even minerals in the Earth are souls and these souls vibrate at the first density level. I wish to repeat that if a soul is to graduate from third density to fourth density then they must have completed the choosing. This means they must have established themselves as either wanting service to self (negative polarity) or else offering service to others (positive polarity).

Here is a description of all seven densities of consciousness:

First Density- Beingness/Awareness
- All organic matter- coal, iron ore, aluminium, quartz, all minerals in the Earth.
- Timeframe in the first density for each incarnation is **billions of years.**

Second Density- Growth/Movement
- All biological life and organic matter with autonomous movement.
- Microbial life through to plants and animals.
- In the later stages of second density, some souls incarnate as pets who benefit from interactions with human beings and develop self-awareness and experience love for their carer.
- Timeframe in the second density for each incarnation is **1-200 years.**

Third Density- Self Awareness/The Choosing
- Most human beings on Earth are at this level.
- This is the shortest of all the densities.
- This is the most difficult of all the densities because of the psychological suffering we experience. This suffering is what forces us to evolve higher.
- During this density we forget who we are and what is going on because of the veil of forgetting.
- During this density we must choose which polarity we want (service to self or service to others).
- To progress to the next density, we must have completed the choosing.
- Timeframe in the third density for each incarnation is **75-100 years.**

Fourth Density- Love and Understanding
- The focus is learning to love and learning selflessness.

- Earth shifted to fourth density in 2012 (most souls on Earth are still third density beings but a growing number are now fourth density beings who have completed the choosing.
- Many later fourth density beings have a combination of a chemical and light body.
- Jesus Christ when he incarnated on Earth in the first century was a later fourth density being. He was what is described as "a wanderer." A wanderer is an advanced being who goes backwards for one incarnation with a specific mission to help that world. Jesus incarnated on Earth in the first century when Earth was a third density planet. He was able by modelling behaviour and through teaching to help push humanity forward in terms of its evolution.
- Earth has only just passed the threshold to be a fourth density planet. This event was foreseen by the Mayan civilisation and calendar which touted 2012 as being the year in which Earth graduates.
- On planets which are more established in fourth density, the beings living there form small groups and are able to actually join minds to create what is called a social memory complex. Communication is telepathic.
- Those souls who have chosen service to self, exhibit extreme hate and narcissism.
- Timeframe in fourth density for each incarnation is **90,000 years.**

Fifth Density- Wisdom and Light
- The body is entirely made of light.
- The focus is on wisdom.
- In the previous fourth density souls can become too focused on love for others to the point of martyrdom. This propensity to neglect oneself is balanced here in the fifth with the attribute of wisdom.
- Lessons of worthiness and unity are learned here.
- Psychic abilities flourish in this density.
- Fifth density beings have powers enabling them to **teleport, manipulate consciousness and to create matter out of thought**.
- Ra does not detail how long the timeframe is for each incarnation.

Sixth Density- Unity/Balance of Love and Wisdom
- The focus is on finding the perfect balance of love and wisdom. Love is an attribute which comes from the feminine whilst wisdom comes from the masculine. At sixth density the balance of divine feminine and divine masculine is achieved.
- Beings which have chosen the negative polarity (service to self) cannot progress past this point unless they reverse their polarity.
- Sixth density beings at this stage act as the higher self for previous versions of themselves at the lower densities. **This means that your higher self is you from the future (sixth density).**
- Timeframe in sixth density for each incarnation is **75 million years.**

Seventh Density- The Gateway
- This is the final density. Beings at this very highly evolved density can be said metaphorically to have one foot in the seventh density and one foot in divine source. At the end of this density, all personal identity will be lost as seventh density souls absorb into the all.
- Seventh destiny beings serve as guides to the higher selves in the sixth density.
- Because Ra has not yet achieved this density there is less information to share. Ra did not say how long each incarnation is.

Ending Thoughts

This is what is going on here in our multiverse which is really an extraordinary computer game. It is indeed mind blowing in its perfection and its design. There are all these steps along the way, and we are only just getting going. We are still in school. Most of us are still at grade 3 or 4. We are a long way away from finishing our PHD in life mastery. But we have an infinity of time to make progress. In fact, we cannot help but make it all the way to seventh density and then merge back with the all. It's impossible not to. If you don't make much progress in this life it doesn't matter because you can play again anytime you want. Remember this is not our home. Our home is the spirit world and I am very sure it's pretty remarkable there!

Once we complete seventh density we become the supreme God. We will bask in pure love and joy with infinite power. This will be the most glorious experience imaginable. No one can know what this may feel like. We become love itself. We will remain as the supreme God as long as we want before we split off again as a new soul and enter a new game. This new game could be radically different to the game we are playing now. At the end of that game we go again in yet another game. Life is like this, cycle after cycle for infinity.

This universe is a computer simulation and that includes us. We are holograms just like everything else in a holographic universe. Don't let this worry you though because the hologram of you is not the real you. You are the entire multiverse. You are consciousness itself or if you prefer you are God and you can't do much better than that can you?

If you come to really believe what I have just written above then you will become enlightened and then life starts to be incredibly fun. You won't have a care in the world and that's the way life is meant to be. So I wish you good luck on your journey. Master those truth bombs and watch how your perception of the game dramatically changes. You don't have to suffer. You can live whilst feeling pure joy. You will be truly happy and content. You will have the peace of Christ.

What would happen to your life if you made a firm decision? That is "I refuse to suffer anymore!" Every time you feel hurt, **refuse to take it personally** and see it through the big picture. It's not that hard. Draw a line in the sand and say "enough to suffering." **This is how you let go of personhood.** This is how you become spiritually enlightened.

It is utterly beautiful this life we are leading. It is rich and deep. We experience deep sadness at times and at other times we can experience utter joy. It is all part of an incredible divine plan. How could life be any more perfect than this! All any of us want is to be happy. All we can want is to wake up each morning excited to see what the day brings.

Remember there is only one of us here doing this. You are God and there is only one God. You have planned this whole thing out and now you are living it. The fact that you are reading this book means you are on the verge of fourth density. Or maybe you are there already. Nevertheless, you have come a long way. This life is beautiful. What a joy to be part of it all.

I hope that you can take some wisdom from this book. I hope it can uplift you. I have tried to write a book that explains what the heck is going on here. Hopefully you can now see the big picture at play. Everything is perfect. Nothing has gone wrong. You are on the right track. I hope that you live well. I hope you experience life deeply. Live every moment. Walk tall and walk forward. You have this.

I will end with a beautiful quote from the indigenous culture of New Zealand, the Maori:

"Turn your face to the sun and the shadows fall behind you" **Maori proverb**

Appendix

State saturation process

When we allow ourselves to fully feel a certain state, we are in the process of re-creating ourselves. As we go about our day, we are usually feeling a real mix of emotions. This makes us feel a real mixture of negative and positive states from moment to moment. This process is about cutting through that jumble of feelings and emotions with a strong and clear message to the universe. We are choosing a state and putting it on steroids so to speak. We are going to turn it up so high that it cuts through and changes our life. This process starts with the conscious mind. It does after time then seep through into the subconscious.

I'm going to use the example of the state of self-love as this is so important to our well-being. I just want to note that this process is targeted at the individual self. I have written about the importance of transcending the belief you are an individual self but as I said in Chapter 5, sometimes we must walk before we can run. We must develop the person to a point before we can transcend believing we are a separate person.

This process requires feeling the state of self-love (or another state of your choice) and turning it right up and holding it. Over time this is enough to change you at the DNA level. The power of the state saturation process is that it changes you at the quantum level. Your cells will start to hold this self-love inside, within the cell. It also re-wires your brain and forms new neural connections.

It seems so simple, and it is easy to do yet this belies just how powerful this process is. Self-love is a great state to start with for anyone as it is an area where a lot of people are lacking. Feeling self-love can change your life significantly. But this process can be used in the same way with emotions or states such as:

  – Worthiness
  – Confidence
  – Self-assuredness
  – Love
  – Contentment
  – Serenity
  – Any other emotion or state you wish

Let's go through the steps in this process now.

Step 1 - Sit down in a chair and close your eyes. Feel the feeling of self-love now (or another state if you are doing something other than self-love).

Step 2 - Now turn this feeling of self-love up. Imagine turning up an imaginary volume control on a phone. Turn it to full volume. Imagine an old-fashioned radio and turn this up to full volume too. Lastly imagine a TV set and turn up the volume of this to full volume. With self-love now pulsating through your body hold it there for 30 seconds, actually feel the self-love. Love yourself right now as hard as you can and hold that feeling. It feels really good!

Step 3 - Assign a colour to this feeling of self-love. Visualise in your mind your whole body being filled up with this colour while you continue to feel as powerfully as you can self-love. Keep this visualisation going for another 30 seconds. Imagine your cells being filled up with self-love at the quantum level. Imagine the neurons in your brain forming new connections.

Step 4 - Imagine now lowering yourself into a hot tub. The water is hot and bubbling. The water is the same colour you have just chosen. Imagine you are bathing in a hot tub of pure self-love. Feel the self-love fully. Imagine yourself completely immersed in self-love. Imagine the hot tub bubbling away around you. Every cell in your body is being filled up with self-love at the quantum level. Do this for 1 minute.

Frequency - Three times a day for two weeks or until the state is established.

Note: Don't be fooled by how very simple this process is. It is incredibly powerful.

Limiting belief blaster

We all hold limiting beliefs in our subconscious mind and these beliefs can sabotage us in our lives. We wonder why things never seem to work out the way we want them too. The problem is we want something with our conscious mind but unfortunately the subconscious mind has other ideas.

We are creating our lives by our thoughts, words, and actions all the time. What many of us don't realise is that the subconscious mind is a very big part of the creation process. If the subconscious mind is not congruent with what we desire with the conscious mind, then we are going to get mixed results.

Science tells us that 95% of the brain's activity is subconscious. This means most of the decisions we make, the actions we take, our emotions and behaviours, depend on the 95% of brain activity that lies beyond conscious awareness. So, if you are wanting a specific outcome with your 5% worth of conscious mind then that is not a lot of creative force if the other 95% of your mind is not onboard.

So, what can we do about something that is beyond our conscious awareness? Luckily, we can do something. This process is the most direct way I have come across. It goes straight to the root of the problem and removes it. All we need to do is have enough self-awareness or intuition to know where we might be tripping up.

This process is a very quick way to clear limiting beliefs we hold in our subconscious mind. It only needs to be done once although repeating the same process every few months will make it even more powerful. We literally hold thousands of limiting beliefs so this process can be used many times. Some of these beliefs are stronger than others. Sometimes just one really entrenched limiting belief can cause us a huge amount of pain and distress in life. Often just removing one limiting belief like this can change our results instantly.

Here are some examples of common limiting beliefs. I've included a lot of examples because limiting beliefs can be anything. You can get really specific with this process. There will be certain things in your life that are unique to you that you could clear. It just takes a bit of self-awareness.

- I am not good enough.
- I don't deserve money.
- I am not very interesting to talk with.
- I will never find a partner.
- I might fail if I change my career.
- I am not smart enough.
- I don't have enough time.
- I am not talented enough.
- I am too .... (old, young, fat, skinny, ugly, tired, dumb, boring etc).

Let's go through the steps in this process now.

Step 1 - Stand up straight and close your eyes. Bring your limiting belief into your conscious mind. Imagine your body now being filled with light. Imagine this light is eradicating all this limiting belief out of your body. It is absorbing the limiting belief, freeing you from it.

Step 2 - Now choose a colour and in your mind's eye, see this light in your body becoming this colour as it continues to suck out the limiting belief from your cells at the quantum level. Do this for 20-30 seconds.

Step 3 - Imagine this coloured light moving from all parts of your body and congregating itself in your belly. Imagine a ball of coloured light, now in your belly.

Step 4 - Imagine a worm hole in space and time opening up 5 metres in front of you. This is a worm hole into another universe. Now imagine the ball of coloured light shooting out of your belly straight into the worm hole, disappearing inside of it.

Step 5 - Turn your head 90 degrees to one side. Imagine you are now looking at the worm hole from the other side. Imagine a backdrop of dark space. You are further back from the worm hole now. See a worm hole open up in the backdrop of space. It is a large opening.

Step 6 - See that ball of coloured light that left your body and went into the worm hole now come shooting out from the other side you are on now. Imagine it shooting right out of the worm hole into the darkness of space in a different universe. (Repeat this step 6 - three times).

Note: This process can be performed many times. It is so quick and easy to do and that is the beauty of it. I have used this process literally thousands of times. I used it 2 or 3 times every day for a period of 3 years initially and I still use it regularly. I literally stripped myself of so many limiting beliefs. You can get really specific on what you want to change. This process just by itself changed me from someone who was a victim in life to someone who was at cause, confident and positive. I don't recommend doing more than three processes a day because sometimes when you clear a limiting belief that is quite entrenched, it may bring to the surface some negative emotions like anger. This is normal and it does not usually last very long. These emotions must be released and that's why they might come to the surface. If this happens to you, take that as an indication that you have successfully removed that limiting belief.